BY JOVE!

ALSO BY MICHAEL MACRONE

• • •

Brush Up Your Shakespeare!

It's Greek to Me!

BY JOVE!

BRUSH UP YOUR MYTHOLOGY

MICHAEL MACRONE
ILLUSTRATIONS BY TOM LULEVITCH

PAVILION

First published in Great Britain in 1993 by
PAVILION BOOKS LIMITED
196 Shaftesbury Avenue, London WC2H 8JL

Text copyright © Cader Company, Inc. 1992
Illustrations © Tom Lulevitch 1992

Created by Cader Books, New York

Published by arrangement with
HarperCollins Publishers, New York

A CIP catalogue record for this book is available from the
British Library

ISBN 1 85793 120 3

Printed and bound in Great Britain by
WBC, Bridgend, Mid Glam.

2 4 6 8 10 9 7 5 3 1

This book may be ordered by post
direct from the publisher. Please contact
the Marketing Department.
But try your bookshop first.

CONTENTS

LIST OF ILLUSTRATIONS

Acknowledgments

Among the many literary and scholarly works I consulted for facts and fictions, a few were especially useful. For information on English usage, I relied on the second edition of *The Oxford English Dictionary* (1989). My basic guides through the cultures and myths of ancient Greece and Rome were *The Oxford Classical Dictionary* (1949); *The Oxford Companion to Classical Literature* (1937); *Dictionnaire de la Mythologie Grecque et Romaine*, by Pierre Grimal, 2nd edition (1958); and the somewhat antiquated but very thorough *Classical Dictionary* by Sir William Smith, revised by G. E. Marindin (1909).

I found detailed and comprehensive summaries of Greek myths, along with edifying commentary, in H. J. Rose's classic *Handbook of Greek Mythology* (1959) and Robert Graves's *Greek Myths* (1955). I recommend these works to readers seeking a fuller account of classical mythology.

My principal literary references were Richmond Lattimore's translations of the *Iliad* (1951) and the *Odyssey* (1967); R. M. Frazer's text of Hesiod's *Theogony* (1983); and A. D. Melville's rendering of Ovid's *Metamorphoses* (1986).

I should like, finally, to thank Michael Cader of Cader Books, along with Hugh Van Dusen and Stephanie Gunning of HarperCollins, for their continuing support.

INTRODUCTION

Though myths have become popular all over again, they never really went away. True, Zeus's infidelities and Hercules' heroics haven't been dinner-table topics for quite some time. But such ancient Greek and Roman tales have enlivened English speech for centuries—in fact, you probably invoke at least one god a day.

It's no secret that fascinating expressions such as "Sisyphean task," "Pandora's box," and "Midas touch" come straight out of classical legend. And it doesn't take a genius to recognize in "aphrodisiac," "mercury," and "dionysian" the names of ancient deities. But you may not know that "fascinating" and "genius" derive from mythical spirits, that "money" is named after the goddess Juno, and that in the original tale, Midas's touch brings him misery, not bliss.

Even if you think mythology is merely a "panacea," a "chimera," a "trivial" "enthusiasm," you can't deny that it's a "cornucopia" of English words and phrases. But don't "panic": this book will guide you through the amusing, profound, and, yes, "tantalizing" stories behind some of our most common expressions. Both a collection of word histories and a primer of classical myth, *By Jove!* will let you explore the hidden meanings of everyday expressions as you brush up your mythology. You're free to seek out archetypes if you wish, but you're also free to simply enjoy yourself.

A BRIEF HISTORY OF MYTH

To the ancient Greeks, *mythoi* simply meant "words" or "tales"; any story, whether legendary, historical, or improvised, was a "myth." Some tales happened to involve gods or heroes, some both, some neither. Whether any of these was "true" was not especially important, at least not by our standards of truth.

Myths weren't invented to please scientists, historians, or philosophers—who repaid the favor by branding them absurd delusions or, at best, clever allegories. Most myths were simply attempts to imagine, in terms of common religious beliefs, how the natural world took shape and why it behaved as it did. Some myths were linked to particular ritual practices, explaining their purpose and meaning. Others, now called "legends," celebrated the great deeds of a clan's patriarchs and heroes. None of these tales had to be proved; their purpose was to offer a satisfying story, not a correct analysis. None was engraved in stone (though a few were painted on vases), and each tended, like the whispered rumor, to grow more fantastic with the telling.

There were neither sacred books of myths nor, in Greece at least, a body of authorities to reconcile and interpret them. In fact, practically every region, if not every settlement, once had its own particular myths. But as clans migrated and mixed, as Greece was invaded in the third and second millennia B.C., and as trade spread throughout the Mediterranean, local myths were modified and combined to incorporate new gods and broader sweeps of place and time. Goddess-worshiping native cultures were conquered by foreign patriarchies; Asian cosmology was imported along with metals and spices; and monsters from abroad crossed paths with local champions. The result was a common pantheon of capricious, anthropomorphic gods who camped on Mount Olympus and pursued their separate interests on earth.

This Olympian mythology was finally recorded and codified by the poets Homer and Hesiod, the former in his legends of Bronze-Age Greek heroes (the *Iliad* and the *Odyssey*) and the latter in his philosophical genealogy of gods and monsters (the *Theogony*). These works of the eighth century B.C. finally gave structure to the fluid and fragmented tales of oral tradition. At the same time, by fixing and solidifying what had been provisional and elusive, they opened myths to interpretation and criticism. Plato, for one, did not like what he saw—Homer's gods were simply not very moral.

But Homer was a poet, not a historian or moralist. He freely revised old myths and invented new details to suit his poetic purpose, and he did not shy from pointing out that Zeus often behaved badly. Homer was neither the first nor the last to tinker with tradition; historians and philosophers would do the same a few centuries later. Every age, in fact, has reinvented old myths in line with its new sensibilities, turning them into romances or satires, demonic histories or heavenly allegories.

So even as major characters and events are more or less fixed, many myths have come down to us in several versions, not all of them compatible. Taking my cue from Homer and Hesiod, I have emphasized particular details and dropped others, selecting the most famous or amusing version of a tale, sometimes incorporating bits of others. I don't pretend to have exhausted any one myth, nor to have offered a complete picture of ancient mythology. With English usage as my guide, I've assumed the mythologist's privilege.

Though this book deals with both Greek and Roman mythology, what is mythical in Roman myths is almost entirely borrowed from Greece. Roman gods were at first just disembodied powers who, though they caused events, had no stories, no history, and no clear relationship to one another. Through commerce and conflict with Greece, the Romans would adopt the anthropomorphic pantheon, but give their own gods' names to the leading actors. (Various other gods and myths would later arrive from Egypt and Asia.)

Eventually, Roman writers added their own details and bent Greek mythology to their own ends; by the time of the empire, they did so mostly for literary or political purposes, as in the works of Virgil and Ovid. Ovid's *Metamorphoses*, a tongue-in-cheek compendium of hoary tales and novel inventions, proved especially influential in later times. It was a big hit during the Renaissance, when Europeans rediscovered classical literature and mythology, and it became a favorite source for literary allusions and adaptations, such as Shakespeare's poem "Venus and Adonis." Whatever the source, myths once again entertained English readers, and over the next four centuries a whole host of gods, goddesses, heroes, heroines, and monsters would make their way into the English language. And they would stay there even once the stories had been forgotten.

ORGANIZATION OF THE TEXT

The body of this book is divided into six sections, each dealing with a separate group of fantastical beings and objects.

The first two sections introduce a variety of gods and spirits, from Chaos to Fortune, while the third and fourth take up the tales of mortals and monsters. The fifth section explores the mythological nomenclature of strange objects, places and states of being, while the last compiles lists of everyday things—including every day of the week—named after mythical characters.

Each section is broken down into entries keyed to an English word or phrase. The first, "Titans and Gods," is arranged according to the gods' age and/or status, making it particularly suitable for a straight reading. I recommend this to those who would like a broad outline before tackling the more diffuse myths and legends recorded in later sections, which are arranged alphabetically. And if you need a quick gloss on the major *dramatis personae*, I refer you to "The Pantheon," appended to the "Mythological Lists" section and beginning on page 220.

BY JOVE!

TITANS AND GODS

Chaos

According to the poet Hesiod, a leading expert on such matters, the first "power" in the universe was a vast, dark void known in Greek as *Chaos* (from *chaino*, "to gape, yawn"). Exactly what kind of void it was is difficult to say. Chaos was the source of the first proper beings—among them Gaia (Earth), Eros (Love), and Nyx (Night)—and Hesiod likely believed, as the philosophers would say, that "nothing comes from nothing"; thus Chaos could not have been mere empty space. More likely it was fancied a diffuse mass of disorganized stuff, matter without form.

This notion recalls the Biblical creation story. We learn from Genesis that the earth was in the beginning "without form, and void; and a darkness was on the face of the deep" (King James Version). But whatever "earth" means here, it is neither alive (like Gaia) nor (while chaotic) born out of Chaos—God creates it. In the Greek myth, Chaos is a great originating force; in the Bible, chaos has to be tamed and shaped by the Creator.

The Greeks were not especially fond of Chaos; it was the great achievement of their supreme god, Zeus, in fact, to establish firm rule over disorderly primal forces and beings. Still, in the Christian tradition the idea of chaos proved more frightening. Though the word "chaos" was first used in English in its root Greek sense—meaning "a great gulf or void"—from the Renaissance on it connoted "confusion, lawlessness, or anarchy." Thomas Hobbes, for example, gloomily predicted in *Leviathan* (1651) that if men did not submit themselves to their Christian sovereign, then all law would be destroyed and "all Order, Government, and Society" would be reduced "to the first Chaos of Violence, and Civil war."

MOTHER EARTH

While "mother earth" traces back to the Latin *Terra Mater*, the Romans were hardly the first to stumble upon this idea, familiar to most ancient cultures. To the Greeks, Earth, a great living ancestor of their gods, was known as Gaia—whence the "Gaia hypothesis," a currently popular conception of the earth as organism rather than as mere object.

Hesiod, borrowing from Eastern mythology, describes Gaia as the first child of Chaos and the mother of various immortals, including the sky-god Uranus, the Titans, the Furies, and the Gigantes. Gaia was generally neutral in the various squabbles among her children and grandchildren, but she played a key role in overthrowing her first child, Uranus [*see* TITANIC, p. 6]. The rest of the time, she just lay around being fertile.

Neither Gaia nor her Roman counterpart Terra has left much of an impression on English literature, but the personification survives in "mother earth," a phrase first used by the Countess of Pembroke in a 1586 translation, ironically enough, of Psalm 146. Though usually written in lower case to blunt the pagan association, "Mother Earth" was given initial capitals in the eighteenth century when applied to a sandy sort of clay or loam.

TITANIC

The Greek gods may have been awe-inspiring, but they were pretty hard to like; time and again they proved as nasty, violent, and power-hungry as mortals. They didn't have much respect for their elders, either—at least not at first, after Uranus (the Sky) mated with his mother Gaia (the Earth) to produce the so-called Titans, the first generation of true gods.

These Titans—Oceanus, Coeus, Crius, Hyperion, Iapetus, Theia, Rhea, Themis, Mnemosyne, Phoebe, Thetis, and Cronus—were grandchildren of Chaos, and there was a distinct family resemblance. Crafty Cronus was both the youngest and the most rambunctious, and as Hesiod tells us, he "despised his lusty father." There was no love lost between Uranus and Gaia, either; things got so bad that one day Gaia fashioned an iron sickle and presented it to Cronus, in effect inviting him to act out his violent fantasies. Cronus took the hint, proceeding to castrate his father, who was then easily deposed by the rest of the Titans.

Not pretty, but it gets uglier. By his sister Rhea, Cronus fathers six children; but, having been warned by his parents that one of these will depose him just as he deposed Uranus, Cronus gobbles down each child as it is born. Only the last, named Zeus, whose birth Rhea takes pains to conceal, is spared this fate [see A CORNUCOPIA, p. 182]. Crafty as Cronus is, he gullibly swallows the swaddled stone Rhea feeds him instead and is none the wiser, though his heartburn must have been terrible.

Zeus, therefore, comes of age on Crete rather than in his father's stomach, and meanwhile Rhea slips Cronus an emetic that induces him to vomit up his other children. One thing leads to another, and upon Zeus's return the younger gods wage war on the Titans. It takes ten years, but the gods do prevail; Zeus then banishes the whole crowd to their own private hell, called Tartarus, in the depths of the underworld.

This victory did not, however, put an end to Zeus's troubles; he still had to face down certain brethren of the Titans, the so-called Gigantes (Giants), mighty savages who sprang from the blood Uranus shed on Gaia after his surgery. Zeus and the other gods defeated the Gigantes, too, in a second legendary war that somewhere along the line got confused with the first. This is how the English words "titan" and "titanic" came to mean "giant" and "colossal" (they once implied "rebellious" too).

You can bet that whoever named that British ocean liner the *Titanic* wasn't thinking of the Titans' disastrous rebellion, but only of their alleged bulk. And when the vessel sank in 1912, the myth went down for good—"titanic" is now rather more likely to recall the catastrophe than the Titans. Not that common parlance is necessarily the poorer, since a number of amusing metaphors have arisen in the liner's wake. The campaign manager of President Gerald Ford's doomed reelection bid in 1976, for example, coined a now-popular phrase when he noted with gloom that he wasn't simply going to "rearrange the furniture on the deck of the *Titanic*."

OLYMPIAN

The original "Olympians" were the third generation of Greek immortals: namely Zeus and the other children of Cronus. These gods take their collective name from Mount Olympus, where they settled after expelling the Titans from the heavens.

In fact many mountains in the ancient world were called "Olympus," but the gods' home was that Olympus located at the eastern end of a long mountain range dividing Greece from its northern neighbor Macedonia. Over 9,500 feet tall and thus the highest peak on the peninsula, its snow-capped summit (thought to touch the heavens) was hidden from view by a wall of clouds, whose gates were secured by the Seasons (minor weather-deities). The Greeks also fancied that, if Zeus and the other gods lived there, the peak must be a place of eternal spring; but believe me, its no place you'd really want to spend a winter vacation.

Olympus should not be confused with Olympia, located on the Peloponnesian plain, which was the site and namesake of the original Olympic Games. Since a great altar consecrated to Zeus had been erected there, perhaps Olympia was named in honor of Olympus; indeed, the word "Olympian" once referred to both places, and may still refer to the games. But far more commonly "Olympian" means "god-like," and more particularly "majestic" or "aloof."

SATURNALIA

THE GOLDEN AGE · SATURNINE · CHRONOLOGY

The Romans were clever, bold, unmatched in combat, and supreme at road-building. But their gods were deadly boring—at least until they appropriated the Greek pantheon, more or less whole, and proceeded to assign Greek myths to native deities. In most cases the translation was smooth, but the Romans had some trouble reconciling their old harvest god Saturnus (Saturn) to his Greek counterpart Cronus.

The Saturn they knew was wise and temperate, unlike Cronus, who was crafty, rebellious, and given to cannibalism [see p. 6]. This myth therefore required some rigging. Conceding that Saturn had castrated his father and eaten his children, the Romans engineered a happy ending: once deposed by Jupiter (their Zeus), Saturn wandered the world repenting of his errors, finally finding refuge in Italy, where he was taken in by Janus, another elder god [see p. 12].

Resolving to make up for past misdeeds, Saturn camped on the Capitoline hill (later site of the Roman citadel) and set about taming the rude natives. He laid down an ethical code and taught the Latins agriculture—though they had little real use for the latter, since the earth brought forth its fruits without any coaxing. Spring was eternal, peace was secured, no need went unmet, labor was unheard of, and health insurance was cheap. This peaceful and prosperous era would be nostalgically regarded as Italy's "Golden Age."

The myth having thus been ironed out, the Romans built Saturn a temple at the foot of the Capitoline and named the last day of their week in his honor [*see* p. 209]. They also celebrated a week-long mid-December festival called Saturnalia, which aside from the occasional human sacrifice was great fun—topsy-turvy, slaves became their masters' masters, and everyone thoroughly debauched himself. (Such liberties were perhaps intended to recall the universal freedom and equality of the Golden Age.)

Englishmen, however, regarded this business as heathen savagery, so they used the word "Saturnalia" (which first appeared in the eighteenth century) to mean "a licentious riot." They rarely noted that the Roman festival, which ended on December 24, in fact inspired several beloved Christmas rituals, such as decking halls and giving gifts.

In Roman statuary, Saturn was represented as an old man, sometimes carrying a sickle in association with the harvest. In this respect he resembles modern depictions of Father Time, and perhaps this is no accident. The name "Cronus," or "Cronos," is very close to the Greek word *chronos*, "time." If Cronus was not originally time personified he later took on that aspect. (The pun may help explain why he ate his children, since, as the proverb goes, "time devours all things.")

Saturn's name was also given by ancient astronomers to the seventh planet, which they thought the outermost. It was believed that since the planet was so distant from the sun and its motion so sluggish, it must transmit cold and gloomy properties to those born under its influence. So in about the fifteenth century Englishmen coined the term "Saturnine temperament." This astrological theory also spawned the epithet "saturnine" for the heavy metal lead; thus those who suffered lead poisoning were called "saturnic."

JANUS-FACED

"Janus-faced" is a now just a fancy way of saying "hypocritical"; but while it's true that Janus was two-faced, the allusion is really unfair. One of the oldest and most dignified of Latin gods, Janus applied himself not to deceit but to guarding households, in particular their doorways. One face inspected those who entered; the other bade farewell to those who left. He thus ensured domestic security and the safety of passages.

For a while Janus grew in power and importance. He became the god of all thresholds, and as the Latin community established the city of Rome he handled the security of its gates and ports. As the god of passages, he also protected birth, the first great passage of life, and soon presided over all beginnings, including that of the year. This is why the Romans gave his name to the first month in their new calendar: *Januarius* [see p. 209].

It was all downhill from there. The Greeks had no equivalent god, so when the Romans assimilated Greek myths Janus lost some face. He was demoted from elder god to mere king, ceding most of his status to Saturn (now identified with the Greek god Cronus), whom Janus was said to have welcomed to Italy. Janus's earlier function as threshold god was then explained by the new story that he had been deified after death and promoted to heaven's gatekeeper—a sloppy patch-up job, at best.

It's certainly appropriate that this two-faced Roman god should have led a double life, but in neither case was he at all hypocritical. In early English writings, Janus was in fact depicted as a pretty good guy; we owe the wholly negative modern use of his name to a certain Anthony Ashley Cooper, third earl of Shaftesbury, who wrote in his *Characteristicks of Men, Manners, Opinions, Times* (1711) of the "Janus-face of writers, who with one countenance force a smile, and with another show nothing beside rage and fury." The damage, despite a few feeble attempts at rehabilitation, had been done. Calling someone Janus-faced today is liable to provoke rage and fury, unless both of you have brushed up your mythology.

AN ATLAS

Chicken Little would have had a lousy time in ancient Greece—most folks were *already* scared stiff the sky was about to fall. When it never did, the notion arose that something must be propping it up—probably that titanic mountain glimpsed in the west, where the heavens meet the earth.

If something held up the sky, then certainly (thought the Greeks) Zeus must have put it there. And that something, according to the logic of myth, must once have been a someone, and someone who offended the god dearly. Any one of the Titans [*see* p. 6] was a good candidate, and the Greeks ultimately settled on Atlas, a brother of crafty Prometheus.

It may surprise you that Atlas supported the sky, not the earth as is now often supposed. But Hesiod says "sky," and Hesiod was always right. The error seems to have arisen once ancient scientists proposed that the heavens were spherical. Artists fell into line by depicting Atlas holding a globe.

According to Hesiod, Atlas was just another Titan punished for siding with the losers in a big cosmic war. But this wasn't good enough for some writers. Ovid, for example, makes Atlas the mortal prince of Mauretania, a northwest-African kingdom thought to lie at the edge of the world, and the supposed site of the fabled Garden of the Hesperides, whose apples were golden [*see* p. 190].

One day the hero Perseus, fresh from slaying Medusa [p. 155], passed through Mauretania and begged Atlas for shelter. But the king, recalling prophecies that a son of Zeus would filch his apples, refused. This set Perseus to boil, but the hero was no match for the king in hand-to-hand combat;

so, pretending to offer Atlas a conciliatory gift, he pulled Medusa's head out of his bag instead. Atlas was instantly turned into stone and, it being Zeus's will, grew in size until he reached the heavens. Atlas, in short, became Mount Atlas, or rather the entire Atlas mountain range in Libya.

There are many other versions of the myth, but none of them explains why a book of maps is called an "atlas." The answer lies in a mistake made by Rumold Mercator when publishing a collection of maps in 1595. Mercator thought Atlas shouldered the earth rather than the sky, and he fancied that a picture of the Titan would aptly grace the title page of a book that contained the world and that could easily be carried on one's shoulder. In its 1636 English edition, this book was given the title *Atlas; or, A Geographic Description of the World*, after which "atlas" became a common name for all such collections.

BY JOVE!

Euphemism is sometimes an ironic enterprise. Take, for example, "By Jove!"—a translation of the Latin oath *pro Juppiter*. In sparing their God an offense, Englishmen have given his pagan counterpart, once thought a demon, a new lease on life.

Jove was the Romans' father-god, which is partly the meaning of his other name "Jupiter"—the "-piter" part derives from the Latin *pater*, "father." The first syllable, like "Jove" itself, stems either from the Indo-European root for "god" (related to the Latin *deus*) or from the old Latin root *div-*, "to shine." Either way, Jove was originally regarded as a god of light, as was his Greek precursor Zeus, whose name is etymologically related.

As a shining god Jove ruled the heavens, commanding the stars, the planets, storms, thunder and lightning. Although like the biblical God a divine king, Jove was neither creator of the universe nor the oldest deity. He simply put an end to a series of chaotic civil wars among the immortals, and he was thus revered as the author of cosmic order. Neither the Greeks nor the Romans could think of him as all-powerful, since they would then be unable to explain the existence of evil, misfortune, and strife. Since Zeus/Jove was fallible, subject to the Fates, and often bamboozled or defied by other gods, he could not be held solely responsible when bad things happened to good people.

Furthermore, while Jove attempted to force order on everybody else, he was himself rather disorderly. Once he had conquered the Titans and Gigantes [*see* TITANIC, p. 6], Jove

put his brothers Neptune and Pluto in charge of the seas and the underworld, respectively, and then devoted himself to his pleasures, namely charming young nymphs and boys, to the understandable anger of his last and most famous wife Juno (Hera, to the Greeks). Mortals considered their endless contentions one source of sublunary woe.

So maybe "By Jove!" is not so apt a euphemism for "By God!" after all. Nonetheless, it proved convenient when Roman myths again graced English literature in the Renaissance. The quip first appears in the anonymous play *Appius and Virginia* (1575), which is based on a story told by the Roman historian Livy. Once Shakespeare picked up the phrase for his comedy *Love's Labor's Lost*, its popularity was assured, as was its essentially comic overtones.

MONEY

This may seem hard to believe, but once upon a time people actually did without money. Even in Homer's day, if you had your eye on somebody's slave, the only way to "buy" him was with a couple of cows, or perhaps some shapely axes. Though pieces of metal may have been exchanged on Crete during the Bronze Age, this practice took over a millennium to reach the Greek mainland (in about the eighth century B.C.) by way of Asia Minor, the original home of coinage (coinage of coins, anyway; Homer coined plenty of phrases).

The word "money" itself is of an even later vintage. It traces back to the Latin *Moneta*, an epithet (meaning "she who advises or warns") bestowed on the Roman goddess Juno, Jupiter's wife and protector of women. Exactly why Juno was called Moneta we don't know, but perhaps it is because strange voices heard from her temple on the Capitoline hill warned the Romans of an earthquake and advised them to sacrifice a pregnant sow. Later, according to another story, as the Gauls were invading Rome in 390 B.C., geese sacred to Juno sounded a warning as the enemy attempted to take the Capitoline by night.

In any event, Juno was given the credit for these and other timely counsels, and thus her old temple was replaced in 344 B.C. with a new one called the Temple of Juno Moneta. But there's one more chapter to the story. In 280 B.C., the Epirian king Pyrrhus—he of "Pyrrhic victory" fame—launched an attack on the Italian mainland, and thousands of Roman soldiers were sent out to meet him. The Romans faced numerous difficulties in this campaign, and at one point they feared they were running short on the funds required to sustain it. A few wise heads among them appealed to their trusty counselor Juno, who issued a brief statement to the effect that those who wage war upon just principles would never lack the necessary cash.

The Romans, who assumed that all their wars were just, were naturally delighted by this piece of advice; so they decided that thenceforth all their money should be coined under Juno's auspices. They established a mint in the Temple of Juno Moneta, after which *moneta* came to mean "mint" and eventually "minted coins." Our word "money" derives from the Old French *moneie*, an adaptation of *moneta*, which is also the source of our word "mint," only this time by way of the Germanic version *munita*.

APOLLONIAN

"Apollonian"—now meaning "rational," "orderly," "controlled" or "harmonious"—once meant simply "resembling or pertaining to Apollo," the Greek sun-god, a patron of art, poetry, and music. The term was rarely used before the late nineteenth century, when the German philologist and philosopher Friedrich Nietzsche, in *The Birth of Tragedy* (1872), drew his famous distinction between "Apollonian" and "Dionysian" tendencies in classical Greek art. According to Nietzsche, the Apollonian qualities of restraint, balance, proportion, rationality, and individuality we admire in the best Greek works were only half the story. Apollonian tendencies struggled against Dionysian complements—wild, unrestrained and uncontrollable forces associated with nature, drunkenness, anonymity, and excess [*see* p. 22].

This distinction rests on the idea that Apollo embodied principles of spirituality and higher wisdom—he was not only the sun-god but also a soothsaying god, the patron of oracles. Being wise, he also inspired philosophy (he was Socrates' sponsor) and oversaw Greek law-making. But by no means was Apollo entirely placid or dull; indeed, he could be aggressive, even wild, when in the mood. Barely out of his crib, he slew the notorious Python [*see* p. 166], and he later proved himself quick to smite any fool who dared insult his mother, Leto. Apollo even rivaled his father, Zeus, in chasing after women and boys, though he was more often frustrated.

The friction between father and son led to an incident which helps explain Apollo's patronage of the arts, particularly music. By his lover Coronis, Apollo fathered a mortal son, Asclepius, who was so expert at healing that the Greeks made him patron of physicians. But when Asclepius devised a means of reviving corpses, a jealous and territorial Zeus struck him dead with a thunderbolt.

Apollo was furious; but there was nothing he could do to Zeus, so he slew the Cyclopes who had supplied the weapon [see A CYCLOPS, p. 150]. Zeus retaliated by banishing Apollo to Thessaly, where he was forced to serve as King Admetus's shepherd (thus becoming the patron of that profession), which bored the former sun-god to tears. So Apollo struck a bargain with Mercury, trading his golden shepherd's staff— the famous Caduceus—for an enchanted lyre; Mercury threw a shepherd's pipe into the bargain.

Apollo quickly mastered both instruments and, after devising some charming lyrics to set to his tunes, became the first in a long line of poetic shepherds. He also thus became the special patron of the Muses, though he would have to split the duties of poetic inspiration with his half-brother and rival Dionysus—a fact some of today's cultural guardians would like us to forget, for reasons which should be clear from the next entry.

DIONYSIAN

Like "Apollonian" [see p. 20], the word "Dionysian" was re-defined and popularized by Nietzsche, who linked Dionysus, Greek god of wine and mystical ecstasy, to emotional, intui-tive, sensual, and unrestrained artistic expression. The re-sulting adjective (spelled with a small *d*) is, however, applied less often today to art than to behavior of an unseemly kind, usually drunken or orgiastic, the flipside of our Apollonian rationality.

Dionysus was always a god more of the people than of the cultured elite. For one thing, his devotees were chiefly women, who needless to say were second-class citizens in the ancient world. What's more, these particular ladies (called "maenads," from the Greek for "crazed"), when inspired by the god, would dance about the hillsides in brazen fashion and then proceed to tear apart live animals and eat their bloody flesh. And that's when they were on good behavior.

These festivities, and other celebrations of the god, were known both as "Dionysia" and as "Bacchanalia," after Dionysus's second name, "Bacchus." The god had different names or nicknames in different locales, which suggests that the official Dionysus—a relatively late addition to the pan-theon—was actually a composite of various local deities. Most of these were gods of vegetation and fertility, and Dio-nysus was later associated particularly with the fruit of trees and vines. In time he would be revered for introducing the cultivation of grapes to various Greek settlements and for setting up their first wineries.

As a god of the masses, Dionysus was less powerful and prestigious than his repressive counterpart Apollo, but his legends are a lot more interesting. These begin with the tale of his strange birth, which, like the rest of his life, was something of a trial. As the most famous version goes, Zeus had fallen in love with yet another beautiful nymph named Semele, whom he seduced in a less sneaky manner than usual—he just appeared to her and announced that he was Zeus. Hera inevitably caught wind of her husband's latest adventure and devised a particularly cruel revenge. She appeared to Semele in the guise of a nurse and asked the gossiping nymph to prove that her lover was really Zeus. When Semele faltered, Hera persuaded her to demand that Zeus appear to her in the same divine splendor in which he appeared to his own wife.

The foolish nymph agreed to this plan and, having sworn Zeus to honor one wish, made her demand. Zeus was cha-

grined, but a promise is a promise; and when he appeared in all his unbearable glory, complete with thunder and lightning, Semele was burned to a crisp. Zeus did manage to rescue her unborn child—namely Dionysus—sewing him into his thigh until fit for birth.

Dionysus had no easier a time of it in life; unlike the other gods, he had to travel around the Greek countryside persuading people he really was divine. (Please note the ironic parallel to his mother's death.) Usually this only required showing them how to make wine, but at times Dionysus had to perform extra miracles or break a few heads. The most famous story, as told in Euripides' *Bacchae*, costars the hubristic Pentheus, king of Thebes and by marriage Bacchus's cousin. Pentheus had no stomach for the bizarre antics of his relative's new cult, and he ridiculed the notion that Dionysus was some sort of god. But when Pentheus tried to have Bacchus killed, the god took revenge by putting the idea in the king's head to dress up as a woman and spy on one of the Bacchanalia. Too bad for Pentheus—the maenads, blinded by the god, took him for a wild boar and, led by Pentheus's own mother, tore him to pieces.

From these lovely Dionysian festivals we derive numerous expressions, such as "bacchanal" and "bacchanalia," which now signify inspiration by spirits rather than by spirit. As first used in the sixteenth century, "bacchanal" implied "drunken orgy"—despite the fact that the maenads needed no wine to get worked up. Even Shakespeare distorts reality in referring to a "riot of tipsy Bacchanals" (*A Midsummer Night's Dream*), while his elder contemporary John Stow sneers at "shameless drunken bacchanalian women." As if a body couldn't have a little sober fun.

An Aphrodisiac

Venereal · Venerate · Venom

We owe the word "aphrodisiac" to the sound-alike Greek expression *aphrodisiakos*, "sexual," originally "pertaining to Aphrodite," the Greek goddess of beauty, love, and generation. Where Aphrodite got her name is another story, which Hesiod relates in his *Theogony*.

Noting the resemblance of "Aphrodite" to the word *aphros*, "foam," Hesiod takes us back to the gruesome castration of the sky-god Uranus [*see* TITANIC, p. 6]. After Cronus cast aside his father's severed member, it skipped across the surface of the ocean, scattering foam as it went. From foam and member Aphrodite was born close by the Greek island Cythera. From there she was carried by the winds to Cyprus, where she was received by the Seasons, and whence she ultimately made her journey to Mount Olympus.

Ridiculous as it may seem, this tale is at least a sincere attempt to account for Aphrodite's Eastern origins in terms of Greek myth. Cythera and Cyprus had been Phoenician trading posts, and in fact Aphrodite strikingly resembles Astarte, the Phoenician goddess of the moon and of women. Astarte was thought to govern the tides, menstruation, and the earth's fertility; her association with the seas accounts for Aphrodite's birth out of sea-foam, and her influence over vegetable and human fertility explains Aphrodite's place in the Greek pantheon as the goddess of sexual desire.

That there had already been a Greek goddess of love named Aphrodite is clear from Homer's reference to her in the *Iliad* as a daughter of Zeus and the mother-goddess Dione. But most of the interesting stories told in later times work out better if Aphrodite is no daughter of Zeus. Take the popular myth of her marriage to the ugliest of deities, the lame fire-god Hephaestus, a union forced on her by a jealous Zeus when she refused his advances.

Though she had no choice in her husband, Aphrodite resolved to consort with whomever she pleased. The first and most famous of her affairs involved the war-god Ares; their mutual attraction may have had something to do with Phoenician beliefs that, among other things, Astarte was a militant goddess. As Homer tells the story, Hephaestus was ignorant of his wife's affair until informed of it by Helios (the Sun), who chanced upon the lovers as he was bringing Ares a message. Enraged, Hephaestus stomped off to his smithy, where he pounded out a durable net whose metal threads were invisibly fine. That evening, he spread the net over his own bed and then made a big show of leaving for a night with the boys.

Thinking the coast clear, Ares tripped into Hephaestus's chambers, where Aphrodite awaited his charms. When the two repaired to bed, the fire-god sprang his trap. Apparently only too happy to publicize his shame, Hephaestus called together all the gods to view the ensnared couple, and everyone found the sight rather jolly. Let loose from the net, the chagrined lovers slunk off in opposite directions, Aphrodite retreating back to Cyprus, where in due time she hooked up with another famous lover, Adonis [see p. 95]. Nor did she stop there: her other paramours would include Hermes and the handsome Trojan Anchises, the fathers by her of Hermaphroditus and Aeneas, respectively.

In Roman myth Aphrodite would be identified with the old Latin love-goddess Venus—the famous statue of Venus de Milo is actually a statue of Aphrodite found on the Greek island Melos, now Milo. Venus, in fact, stole most of her ancestor's thunder, especially when it came to English coinages. Even "aphrodisiac," which honors the Greek goddess, was first defined in 1719 as something exciting "Lust or Venery"—and "venery" (a synonym of "lust") is a Venus-derivative. "Venereal," too, is a term considerably older than "aphrodisiac," as it dates to the fifteenth century; the phrase "venereal disease" had already come into use by the mid-seventeenth century.

Oddly enough, Venus's name is also the root of our word "venom," from the Latin *venenum*, originally "love potion, charm" and later "drug, poison." Though the English "venom" also once referred to evil potions generally, this usage all but disappeared by the nineteenth century, leaving only the present meaning. More congenial to the goddess Venus is another derivative, "venerate," from the Latin *venerari*, "to worship or revere," rooted in the equation of Venus with love.

MARTIAL

Where the Greek war-god Ares pulled in negative ratings nearly equal to Hades', his Roman counterpart Mars proved a big favorite in Italy. Of course, the conquering Romans had more to be grateful for, especially since their city's founders, Romulus and Remus, were reportedly Mars's sons. The Greek god's most notable achievement, on the other hand, was to side with the enemy in the Trojan War.

One of the original "big three" (with Jupiter and Janus) among Latin deities, Mars was a god for all seasons, presiding over agriculture in the Romans' agrarian phase and over war in their "martial" phase. Actually, in his former capacity he favored one season in particular, namely spring, and he lent his name to its first month: *Martis*—"March" in English. When Mars relinquished his plowshare to lesser gods in order to take up the sword, this did not require changing his month's name; the Romans also used spring to launch their major campaigns.

It would be neat if the god behind "martial" and "March" also lent us the verb "to march," but etymology is seldom neat. "To march" actually traces from the French *marcher*, "to walk," originally "to trample," itself perhaps from the Latin *marcus*, "hammer." On the other hand, Mars *is* the source of "Martian." Whether or not it was ever home to little green men, the red planet was once thought to agitate earthlings, so that intemperate persons, as well as military men, were called "martial."

Mercurial

The Caduceus · Mercury · Hermetic Hermeneutic

Like "saturnine" and "jovial," "mercurial" once referred principally to planetary influences, even well after people stopped believing planets were gods. Yet the first planet, being closest to the sun and thus fastest in orbit, does rather resemble its Roman namesake Mercury, Jupiter's confidant and speedy envoy.

Originally a patron of commerce (the Latin *merces* means "merchandise"), Mercury assumed his new duties from the Greek god Hermes, who was not only fleet-footed but also quick-witted. Whatever required wit, craft, or agility fell under Hermes' influence, and his attributes ranged from lofty eloquence to thievish cunning.

Reputedly the son of Zeus and Atlas's daughter Maia, Hermes was perhaps a spirit of the roadside in very ancient times, guarding travelers and their goods. Or perhaps he was a spirit of good luck—particularly in raising cattle and in agricultural trade, given his origins in the pastoral region of Arcadia. He had, it seems, a special thing for ruminants. It is said that on the very day he was born, Hermes made his speedy way to Thessaly, where his brother Apollo was playing the shepherd [*see* APOLLONIAN, p. 20]. Already possessed of a fine criminal mind, Hermes raided Apollo's herd, transported a good portion to a secret cave, and sacrificed a brace of oxen to his father, Zeus.

Apollo stormed off to Hermes' mother to lodge a complaint. Maia, however, denied Apollo's accusations, pointing out that the alleged perpetrator, who had already snuck back home, was merely an infant. But Apollo knew better, and so he snatched up the baby Hermes to present him at the court of Zeus. Hermes ultimately confessed and returned the oxen, but Zeus admired the child's cunning and thought he would make a natural diplomat. Hermes thus became Zeus's personal envoy, though his extensive portfolio also required running shades down to Hades' infernal kingdom [*see* GO TO HADES, p. 33].

Still not a day old, Hermes also showed off his skill at invention by taking a tortoise shell and stringing it with the guts of the sacrificed oxen, thereby devising the lyre (the

Greeks' favorite instrument). With this lyre he procured from Apollo a charmed, forked staff called the Caduceus, which made him look just the part of a Greek messenger, along with his broad-brimmed hat and durable sandals. In time these prosaic furnishings benefitted from poetic detailing; Hermes' cap and shoes sprouted wings (to signify his speed), and the two ribbons entwining his Caduceus were transformed into snakes.

The story is that Hermes found these snakes engaged in a brawl, which he used his diplomatic skill to quell, prompting the serpents to wind themselves around his staff. More likely, the Greeks simply adapted an ancient symbol of arcane wisdom (tracing to prehistoric Mesopotamia) to the simple forked olive branch sported by their most learned god. In any case this be-serpented Caduceus became a special emblem of heralds and ambassadors in the ancient world. In sixteenth-century Europe, however, it was transferred to physicians, who confused Hermes' staff with that of the healer Asclepius, though the latter featured but a single snake.

The versatile Hermes and especially his Roman counterpart have lent their names to objects and qualities as wide-ranging as their skills. "Mercurial," for example, may mean almost anything: "eloquent," "quick-witted," "talented in business," or simply "quick to change." The god's speed and volatility also account for the newer name, "mercury," given to a metal known only as "quicksilver" before the fourteenth century.

The Greek god, meanwhile, accounts for two slightly less familiar terms. As the bearer of dreams from Zeus to mankind, Hermes was associated with the imagination, which, along with his rhetorical skill and his invention of the lyre, made him a patron of poetry and of writing in general. The Greeks thus assumed that Hermes was not only Zeus's messenger but also his interpreter, a belief that gave rise, by the early eighteenth century, to the English word "hermeneutic," meaning "interpretative."

More curious is "hermetic," which originally referred to certain mystical and scientific writings attributed to Hermes in his Egyptian manifestation as Thoth. Called "Hermes Trismegistus," meaning "Hermes the Great Great Great," the presumed author was like the Greek Hermes a figment of the imagination, but a figment of a rather later date than some philosophers professed to believe. Medieval and especially Renaissance thinkers supposed this Hermes was the inventor of writing and a contemporary of Moses, that his works were the source of all Greek wisdom, and even that he was inspired by God. But as it turns out the Hermetic texts were written perhaps as late as the fourth century A.D., having been cleverly forged so as to appear of great antiquity.

Though the myth of Hermes Trismegistus was finally and ruthlessly exploded in 1614 by the protestant polemicist Casaubon, the term "hermetical," later simply "hermetic," survived as a term for occult writings, especially treatises on alchemy or magic. (Hermes was big on alchemy.) Since chemistry in its infancy relied heavily on alchemical methods and terminology, when seventeenth-century chemists devised a method for sealing retorts airtight by melting their glass openings, they called this closure the "seal of Hermes" or "hermetic seal." The former term was coined along with the method circa 1605, while the latter appears by the 1660s.

GO TO HADES

"Go to Hades!" may seem innocuous to us, but no ancient Greek would have been caught dead saying such a thing. In the first place, Hades wasn't somewhere you could go, since it was the name of a god; in the second place, uttering his name only made him mad.

One of the elder Olympians, Hades ruled over the Greek underworld, the final home of all "shades" (spirits of the dead), whether good or evil. The underworld, therefore, is not the same thing as hell, nor is Hades a Greek devil. Bounded by the river Styx [see p. 199], Hades' kingdom was a place of utter darkness, which may explain his name—"Mr. Invisible" in Greek. It may also account for a certain helmet given him by the Cyclopes, called the "Cap of Hades," that rendered its wearer invisible.

A shy god, Hades kept to himself, which was all for the best—he was exceedingly grim and not much to look at either. Naturally, no goddess in her right mind would marry him, so Hades was forced to steal a mate. In collusion with her father, Zeus, he settled on the equally charmless Persephone, whom Hades snatched up as she was gathering narcissus flowers (traditionally associated with death—see AN ECHO AND NARCISSISM, p. 55).

It was presumed that Hades, as the underworld god, exerted some influence over the growth and decay of crops—thus his euphemistic nickname "Pluto," from the Greek for "bounty." So Persephone, as daughter of the corn-goddess Demeter, made a fit, if unwilling, companion [see CEREAL, p. 40]. Given her druthers Persephone would have fled Hades' kingdom for good, but the god cleverly fed her pomegranate seeds, which for some reason forced her to live with the dead for a third of the year.

All this chicanery at least kept Hades busy. In the early days of Greek myth, especially, he had little else to do, since when new shades arrived they merely sunk into a stupor. Later on the Greeks decided that shades were rewarded or punished according to their virtue or viciousness, but even then Hades delegated his dirty work to the Furies [see p. 35]. The underworld was then divided into regions of pleasure and pain, and formerly distinct places such as Tartarus and Elysium became neighborhoods in Hades' kingdom.

Whatever the underworld's topography, ancient Greeks never called it "Hades," though you could "go to Hades" in the sense of paying the god a visit. By the time the Hebrew bible was rendered into Greek, however, "Hades" had come to refer to the kingdom rather than to the god, and it was used to translate *sheol*, "the abode of the dead." In this connection, "Hades" was introduced into English late in the sixteenth century, when it figured in a scriptural controversy.

One point of argument was whether Hades was in fact the same place or condition as hell. Whatever the scholars' opinion the common people eventually decided it was. Even better, being a novel foreign import, "Hades" was free of the superstitions surrounding the dreaded word "hell." Thus a name taboo to the Greeks became a euphemism for a name taboo among Englishmen.

THE FURIES

To us, "furies" is a quaint word for violent storms or angry women. But to the ancient Greeks, the Furies were anything but quaint, being personified curses and pitiless agents of vengeance. Since it was said that they arose from the blood Uranus shed on Gaia after his son mutilated him [*see* TITANIC, p. 6], the Furies above all represented a parent's curse upon unkind children, and they most vigorously pursued evildoers who violated the bonds of kin or clan.

The notion of such Furies—"Erinyes" to the Greeks—was vague at first, but already in Homer's work they have two specific jobs: punishing the shades of evil men in Tartarus, and effecting curses on Earth. Later writers decided there were exactly three of them—just as there were three Fates, three Cyclopes, and so forth—and that they were grim, if beautiful, deities clad in black, whose eyes dripped blood, whose hair was tangled with serpents, and whose weapon of choice was the scourge. While they may have literally lashed the "bodies" of evil shades, they tormented the living psychologically—that is, they personified guilt, or at least what approximated guilt in early Greek society.

The most famous myth of the Erinyes has to do with their relentless pursuit of the hero Orestes, a story first presented in detail by the tragedian Aeschylus. After Orestes' mother, Clytaemnestra, joined in the murder of his father, Agamemnon, Orestes paid her back in kind, as was his duty according to the prevailing moral code. But the Erinyes cared not a whit for moral codes; all they knew was that a son had shed

the blood of his mother, and that they were required to torment him. But with Apollo's help, Orestes cleared himself before a jury of his peers—legendarily, the first such jury in history, and the first instance in which motives and circumstances were taken to bear upon judging a crime.

Though Orestes was acquitted, he still took pains to propitiate the Erinyes, as a result of which they supposedly grew milder in character. Thus they earned the euphemistic nickname "Eumenides" ("the Kindly Ones"), a moniker which in truth more likely resulted from a superstitious fear of invoking them by name. The Romans, however, would still regard them principally as raging, vengeful figures, and so when they adopted the trio from Greek myth they dubbed them "Furiae," after the verb *furere*, "to be raging mad." It is from the verb rather than from the goddesses that we derive our words "fury," "furious," and so on, though the plural "furies" retains some hint of the ancient personification.

A Volcano

It wasn't long after the Greeks discovered fire that they figured it must be the gift of some god. But since there are two kinds of fire—good (the cozy hearth-fire) and bad (which burns cities and overcooks your dinner)—they decided there must be two fire-gods as well: one friendly—Hestia, goddess of the hearth; and the other hostile—Hephaestus, god of destructive fire.

While nobody liked Hephaestus very much, it was still his fire rather than Hestia's that made possible such crafts as metalworking. As a result cults sprang up in the more advanced Greek cities. And since any proper cult requires its god to have an amusing history, Hephaestus eventually became the subject of detailed, albeit humble, myths.

If you believe Homer, Hephaestus was a son of Zeus and Hera, and a very ugly son to boot, which endeared him to neither of his parents. By one account (referred to in Plato's *Republic*), Hephaestus, despite Hera's neglect, came to her rescue when a jealous Zeus was about to beat her, prompting Zeus to grab his son by the foot and hurl him from the top of Olympus. It took nine days for Hephaestus to strike ground on the Aegean island Lemnos, but when he did he hit it hard, breaking a leg on impact (it's a miracle he didn't break his neck).

Thus Hephaestus was lamed for life, in this respect resembling many Greek smiths, whose infirmity stuck them with stationary labor. Neither inclined to return home nor really capable of it, Hephaestus toiled in the bowels of Lemnos's volcano, whose smoke and fire were supposed to issue from his workshop. There, with help from the Cyclopes, he fashioned Zeus's thunderbolts and other useful items [see pp. 44, 203].

He also hammered out a little surprise for his ungrateful mother: a devious trap in the shape of a golden throne, which he sent up to Olympus as a gift. Hera, delighted with her son's device, plunked herself down on the throne, only to discover that she couldn't get up again. Even the most muscular gods couldn't pry her off—Zeus probably didn't try all that hard—and everyone soon realized that only Hephaestus could undo the damage he had done. At this point the clever wine-god Dionysus hied himself to Lemnos to get his brother thoroughly drunk and drag him back home, where Hephaestus kissed and made up with his parents.

A fat lot of good it did him, too, since while the gods required his craftsmanship they mostly wanted him around to laugh at. Jokes about his lameness abounded, and everyone was mightily amused when Hephaestus caught his wife *in flagrante delicto* [see AN APHRODISIAC, p. 25]. Whether to flee such ridicule or just to expand his business, Hephaestus would often repair to earth and open new volcano workshops.

The Romans thought Hephaestus, whom they called Volcanus (in Late Latin, *Vulcanus*), had his headquarters within Mount Aetna on Sicily, and that he took the Cyclopes into employment there rather than at Lemnos. Wherever the headquarters, the franchise was extensive; whenever a mountain began belching up fire and ash it was assumed that Volcanus had opened a new branch. These stories later gave rise to the Italian word *volcano* (or *vulcano*), the direct an-

cestor of our word "volcano," spelled "vulcano" when first used in 1613. (Volcanoes had been called "Volcans" or "Vulcans" in the sixteenth century.)

Volcanus also lent his name to the industrial process of tempering india rubber with intense heat, patented in the mid-nineteenth century and dubbed "vulcanization." The hard rubber product was in turn called "vulcanite." It is unclear whether Volcanus himself ever bothered with rubber, but the fact that he toiled within volcanoes inspired the name "vulcanology" for their scientific study.

CEREAL

The next time you feast on a bowl of Cap'n Crunch's Crunchberries, you might pay your respects to Ceres, the unofficial patron goddess of breakfast cereals. Actually, you should probably buy a box of corn flakes, since Ceres was more properly a Roman corn-goddess. Called Demeter by the Greeks, she was, as patroness of agriculture, closely allied with Mother Earth (Gaia), but also with the underworld god Hades, who married her daughter Persephone [see p. 33].

More to the point, Hades *stole* Persephone, which led Demeter to withdraw her powers in a sulk, leaving the earth utterly barren. (This detail may refer to some actual catastrophe.) Luckily, Demeter relented when Zeus contrived her daughter's return, but since Persephone had eaten Elysian pomegranate seeds she was forced to spend a third of the year underground. Since Persephone was a spirit of growth, this explains why harvests are seasonal rather than perpetual, as they had been in the Golden Age.

Deriving from the Latin *Cerealis*, "pertaining to Ceres," the English "cereal" was first used in 1600 by Philemon Holland, translating Livy, with reference to Roman festivals in the goddess's honor. But the word quickly dropped out of sight, only to be revived in nineteenth century, first as an adjective meaning "pertaining to corn or grain" and then as a noun for grain plants.

By 1899, "cereal" had also come to refer more specifically to foods made from processed cereal grains (an advertisement in the *Chicago Daily News* that year offered a "handsomely decorated tea canister" free with six packages of "Hazel Cereals"). Within a decade such products, having become a staple of the American breakfast, were dubbed "breakfast cereals," and within another few decades the fashion had spread to Britain.

Not everyone, however, was pleased. As Mr. Saxby hotly remarks in P. G. Wodehouse's novel *Cocktail Time* (1958), "When I was a young man . . . there were no cereals. We ate good wholesome porridge for breakfast and throve on it. Then along came these Americans with their Cute Crispies and Crunchy Whoopsies and so forth, and what's the result? Dyspepsia is rife. England is riddled with it." On the other hand, if porridge is the alternative I think I'll take Crunchy Whoopsies.

THE THREAD OF LIFE

The image of life as a thread comes straight from the Greek conception of fate. As early as Homer's epics we find references to a Fate or Fates (*Moirai*) who spin out each person's life, though Homer cannot decide whether or not Zeus has any say in their business. Hesiod, though he fudges their genealogy—making them daughters of Night here and of Zeus there—is certain that the Fates are three in number and that their decrees are inexorable. These deities, being relentless, unforgiving, and deaf to all pleas, were routinely called "the Cruel Fates," a Greek epithet still familiar in English.

Of the three, Clotho ("the Spinner") spun out the thread, Lachesis ("the Apportioner") measured and guided it, and Atropos ("the Inflexible") would snip it at the fated moment with a pair of great scissors (thus the notion of a "life cut short"). The Romans liked the idea but not the name "Moirai," which they changed to "Parcae" after the old goddess of childbirth Parca—believing, like the Greeks, that your fate was allotted at birth.

It is from the more general Latin word *fatum* ("that which has been spoken"), however, that we derive our word "fate." Where *fatum* originally referred to any divine decree, in popular Roman religion the plural *Fata* became identified with the Parcae, and a certain goddess named Fata Scribunda was said to preside over childbirth and to write down one's destiny on a heavenly scroll. The Romans must not have thought their Fates so cruel, since they extended the name *fata* to entirely more pleasant spirits—indeed, *fata* is, by way of French, the source of our word "fairy."

PROMETHEAN AND
A PANDORA'S BOX

When Zeus is feeling vengeful, he really goes for it. Take the case of the Titan Prometheus, who according to Hesiod so outrages the gods that Zeus ties him to a column and commands an eagle to eat his liver. Each day the eagle feasts, and each night the liver regenerates. It makes me sick just to think about it.

This is not a tale exactly designed to cast Zeus in a positive light. While it's true that Prometheus, perhaps in origin a fire-god, spent many a day plotting to make fools of the gods, the rest of the time he was mankind's best friend; indeed, according to some he fashioned the first men out of clay. And, to his credit, he taught his mortal progeny the proper uses of fire, invented mathematics, and introduced such crafts as metal-working, architecture, and writing. These achievements, however, only made Zeus more jealous.

The last straw was the Titan's attempt to deprive Zeus of his due from a burnt offering. Prometheus covered up the useless bones in a promising looking lump of fat, hid the good bits under the beast's stomach (the gods didn't go for stomachs), and invited Zeus to choose his share.

Zeus was fooled, and mighty unhappy about it. To forestall future shenanigans, the god deprived mankind of fire, prompting Prometheus to pull his most heroic and most foolish caper. He stole up to Mount Olympus and, when no one was looking, bottled up enough fire in the hollow of a fennel stalk to get things burning again back on earth.

Now Zeus was furious. Since he couldn't actually kill Prometheus—the Titans were as immortal as the gods—he devised the horrifying punishment Hesiod describes. But once Prometheus had writhed in agony long enough—how long the myths don't say—Zeus allowed his son Heracles to kill the eagle. Zeus no longer had Prometheus on his conscience, and Heracles gained a little more glory.

The English word "Promethean," meaning "bold," "crafty," or "original," seems to have been first used by Shakespeare in *Love's Labor's Lost* (1595), in which Berowne boldly claims that women's eyes are the source of "the true Promethean fire" (I suppose he means that loving looks spur a man's achievements). Milton later used "Promethean" to mean "expert in craftsmanship," and thus came closer to the modern sense. When Charles Darwin employed the word in 1845, however, he was referring to a now-obsolete brand of fire-givers: "I carried with me some promethean matches, which I ignited by biting." Ouch.

A PANDORA'S BOX

Once Zeus has taken care of Prometheus, he turns his attention to men, who, having recouped fire, still haven't properly suffered for helping ruin his dinner. Zeus sets about devising a more foolproof retort, which will require a fool to work.

The result is Pandora, a deviously clever imitation of a virgin goddess crafted out of clay by the fire-god Hephaestus. Other gods join in the effort, bestowing Pandora with wifely skills, beguiling charm, sparkling jewelry, a flattering tongue, and an evil heart—everything to drive a man wild. (Thus her name: "pandora" means "all-gifted.") Zeus then packs her off to earth—where there is not yet a single female—and Hermes presents her to Prometheus's brother Epimetheus.

Now Prometheus, whose name means "Foresight," had expected some such ruse, so he had warned his brother not to accept any gifts from Zeus, no matter how nice they might appear. But Epimetheus ("Hindsight") can't resist Pandora's charms; he not only takes the gift, but weds her posthaste.

As it happens, Zeus, preparing his revenge, had earlier sent Epimetheus another "gift," namely a huge jar, complete with instructions that it should never be opened. The nature of this jar Epimetheus could not guess; but, clod though he was, he had the sense not to tamper with it. His new wife, on the other hand, is not only beautiful and wicked, but also insatiably curious; a command to let something be is to her an invitation to meddle.

Thus the terrible beauty of Zeus's plot: inside that jar are stored all the evils from which mankind, in its blessed state, is as yet free; and inside Pandora's heart is a reckless desire.

Off comes the lid, and out spring disease, plague, envy, hatred, and every other bad thing you can imagine, including taxes. Pandora, surprised, slaps the lid back on, but too late: the only thing left in the jar is hope. What hope was doing in there in the first place is difficult to explain, as is the significance of its remaining; nobody's interpretation is terribly convincing, and I'm not even going to try. (In another version, Pandora herself carries the jar of evils to earth, and it is the foolish Epimetheus, rather than the crafty Pandora, who opens it. Though not as neat as Hesiod's version, this one has the virtue of being slightly less misogynistic.)

Two things about this story are particularly interesting. First, the Greeks imagined that women, beautiful outside but evil inside, were created by the gods specifically in order to make men miserable. In this regard, and given the result of her curiosity, Pandora strikingly resembles a certain original woman in the Judeo-Christian creation story.

Second, you will notice that Pandora opens a jar and not a box; Hesiod's word is *pithos*, which refers to a jar for storing grain. We seem to owe the phrase "Pandora's box" to the sixteenth-century humanist Erasmus of Rotterdam, who perhaps confused *pithos* with *pyxis*, "box." (Another of Erasmus's slips yielded "to call a spade a spade"—it's "to call a kneading-trough a kneading-trough" in the original.) Whether or not Erasmus knew what he was doing, Englishmen trusted him in everything. So from the very start it was "Pandora's box," a phrase which has since the sixteenth century metaphorically referred to something which on the outside appears harmless but which, if indulged, causes limitless harm.

LESSER GODS, DEMI-GODS, AND NYMPHS

CUPID AND PSYCHE

To the Greeks, *psyche* meant "the soul," but it's unclear exactly what they had in mind. Perhaps originally thought of as bird-like, by Homer's time the soul was imagined as a person's ephemeral twin, an identical shade or reflection that retired to the underworld once the body had perished. Once there, the soul would waste away in a daze, perking back up only when offered a refreshing cup of blood.

Greek artists, however, favored the more poetic image of the soul as a beautiful young maiden. (Philosophers, too, had decided the soul was female.) Eventually, such generic depictions of *psyche* yielded the myth of Psyche, the soul personified, who was beloved by the love-god Cupid. This is the happy pair that invented the kiss.

The notion that desire loves the soul is certainly abstract, but it inspired a memorable fairy tale, first found in the satirical *Metamorphoses* (a.k.a. *The Golden Ass*) by the Roman wit Apuleius (second century A.D.). In this story Psyche is a princess, the most stunning of three beautiful sisters. She is so breathtaking, in fact, that all the thousands who come to ogle her take her to be a new Venus—even better than the original, in fact, because still a virgin. The true Venus is all but forgotten and her worship abandoned, which of course makes the goddess insanely jealous.

Venus enlists her mischievous son in a campaign of revenge, charging him to drive Psyche into the arms of the vilest man imaginable. But her plot backfires when Cupid himself is smitten by the princess. To make a very long story a little shorter, Cupid orders the West Wind to whisk Psyche down from a mountaintop to a palace he's built for the occasion, where he visits her in darkest night to consummate what he calls their marriage. Psyche is delighted, but Cupid, intent on concealing his identity, warns that should she ever look upon him she will lose him forever.

Meanwhile, Psyche's family begins to wonder what's become of her, and soon her sisters make their way to the mountaintop where she disappeared. At Psyche's command, the West Wind sweeps them down to the palace for a sisterly cup of tea; but after they've sized up Psyche's goddess-like life-style they grow desperately jealous. Though married to kings and pampered to an extreme, once home they fall to bitter complaints, deciding their happiness now rests on destroying Psyche's—or, if necessary, destroying Psyche herself.

So they return, courtesy of the West Wind, to the palace, where, after interrogating the now-pregnant princess, they learn that she's never actually seen her husband. Figuring this must be because he's a god, and that their hated sister will probably die if she dares look at him, they concoct a sort of deadly phallic joke, telling Psyche she's married to a monstrous constrictor snake who's planning to eat her once her pregnancy comes to term. They advise her to procure a lamp and a knife and use them to kill the snake that night.

The gullible Psyche swallows the bait, waiting until Cupid is asleep beside her and then, armed with her knife, shining the lamp upon him. As she realizes her terrible mistake, a drop of oil sizzles from the lamp, burning Cupid's shoulder. The agonized love-god wakes, bawls Psyche out, and then goes crying to his mother.

The desolate Psyche, now exiled from Cupid's palace, wanders aimlessly through Greece, until one day she chances upon the city where her elder sister is queen. Showing uncharacteristic cleverness, Psyche reveals to her sibling that her husband was not a snake, but Cupid, and that the god has divorced her in order to marry her elder sister. The latter, too vain to doubt this news, races off to the old mountaintop and jumps, expecting the usual ride. But the wind is on vacation, and so she is smashed to pieces on the rocky mountainside. Now rinse and repeat with second sister.

These harpies out of the way, the field is clear for the infinitely more dangerous Venus, who, having been apprised of her son's treachery, is thirsty for Psyche's blood. Once Psyche discovers that none of the gods intends to lift a finger in her defense, she decides she'd better try arranging some sort of plea bargain. Venus, however, is in no mood to cut a deal, putting Psyche through a series of deadly trials instead.

Unlike the gods, nature takes pity on the princess, helping her out with various instructions and warnings. Yet just when she's almost in the clear, Psyche blows it. Succumbing to curiosity, she peeps into a box she's fetched for Venus from the underworld; out of the box leaps a deathly sleep that quickly enshrouds her. Just in the nick of time, Cupid escapes from the prison Venus has kept him in, rushes to Psyche's side, and brushes the sleep back into its box.

Taking no more chances, Cupid flies up to Olympus and begs Jupiter to put an end to these shenanigans. Though Jupiter blames Cupid for his own various embarrassing adulteries, he nonetheless proclaims to all the gods that Cupid and Psyche are now lawfully married, and tells Venus to lay off. He palliates the love-goddess by assuring her the match shall not debase her blood, and then bids Psyche to drink some nectar, which instantly makes her immortal [see p. 177]. Soon thereafter, Psyche bears a daughter, named Pleasure, and everyone lives happily ever after.

If there is a moral to the story, which is actually just a glorified folk tale, perhaps it has to do with the soul's purification through suffering, which renders it worthy of divine love. In any case, Apuleius quickly forgot about morals once he got caught up in the details, which was probably all for the best.

A DEMON

In Greek myth, while demons weren't always very nice, they were hardly evil. Nor did they have anything in particular to do with Hades. These demons, rather, were agents employed by all the gods in their dealings with men.

Actually, as Homer describes it, a demon (*daimon*) was the active aspect of a god, a manifestation of his power. Later writers more fully personified this divine aspect, so the *daimones* came to be seen as quasi-divine spirits who shrouded themselves in mists to block prying mortals' vision. These spirits supposedly kept watch over mankind and effected the gods' will vis-à-vis individuals—notions resulting in the belief that each man has a *daimon*, or perhaps two (one good, one evil), entrusted with his fate. This sort of *daimon* is very similar to the Romans' *genius* [see p. 62], although the *genii* were generally a nicer bunch.

Hesiod speculated that there were precisely 30,000 *daimones*, the spirits of those lucky people who had lived during the so-called Golden Age. Administrators of Zeus's judgments, these spirits were in fact gods, but third-rank gods not even dignified with names. As a group, however, they suffered even greater indignities at Christian hands. Even as their novel creed spread across the Hellenistic world, the Christians found the old mythology somewhat intractable; since they could not banish the old gods outright, they persuaded their pagan converts that the Greek pantheon was full of evil spirits rather than gods.

In the process, the Greeks' *daimones* became the English "demons," later used to translate the Hebrew words for

"idols" and "hairy ones" in the Old Testament. In the 1706 edition of Edward Phillips' English dictionary, it is reported that "*Demon* . . . in Holy Scripture . . . is always taken for the Devil or a Bad Genius." However, Englishmen used "demon" in the old Greek sense about as early as they used it in the derogatory new sense, both usages dating to the late fourteenth century.

That the old sense of "demon" survived—and survived until early in this century—had much to do with one very famous *daimon*, supposed to have been Socrates' guiding spirit. Though in Plato's dialogues Socrates never actually mentions having a personal *daimon*, he does claim to be guided by the "divine things," *daimonion* in Plato's Greek. This word was later adapted by the Romans as *daemonium*, "a divine or demonic thing." And from this Latin word and the Greek prefix *pan-* ("all"), John Milton coined the compound "Pandemonium" for the capital city of hell. Milton, being an enthusiast of the idea that the pagan gods were lesser devils in Satan's service, may have used Greek words, but he interpreted them the way the early Christians had.

AN ECHO AND NARCISSISM

According to Ovid, whose version of the Greek tale is now the best known, Echo was once a very chatty nymph, so good at schmoozing that Jove himself was eager to employ her. As we have seen, the supreme god had a weak grip on his libido and he naturally took pains to conceal his adulteries from his wife, Juno. For a while Echo proved a handy and effective shield; as Jove frolicked, Echo would divert Juno with the latest gossip.

The goddess eventually saw through this ruse—as she usually did with Jove's deceptions—and decided to punish Echo in a manner befitting the crime. Juno tied up the nymph's glib tongue, dooming her merely to repeat the final words of others' speeches.

Echo only realized the true cruelty of her fate after falling madly in love with a beautiful young man named Narcissus. Though she aches to impress her feelings upon him, she can only echo tags of the questions he asks. Her repetitions are at last so annoying that Narcissus flees, leaving Echo to pine away until she shrivels into the disembodied voice we now, in her honor, call an "echo."

Echo was hardly Narcissus's sole victim. In fact, everyone who laid eyes on him swore instant devotion, which only swelled the boy's head until nobody, in his opinion, was worth the time of day. His haughtiness only set him up for a fall, however, and Narcissus finally broke one heart too many. After being cruelly scorned, one heartsick youth beseeched the gods to make Narcissus know how it feels to be desperately but impossibly in love. Nemesis—the goddess who ruins the proud [see p. 73]—heeded the call.

One day, when Narcissus happens upon a limpid pool, Nemesis strikes: as the beautiful youth stoops to drink, he glimpses his reflection and is bewitched. Thinking the image real and admiring its godlike figure, Narcissus begins to woo it. Poignantly, the image returns his praise and his longing looks, offers to meet his kiss, burns with the same desire.

At least Narcissus's hapless suitors knew what he thought of them, but the cruel image just leads him on. The teenager pathetically gropes for his lover but just comes up wet; yet the reflection's coy behavior only sharpens his desire. Finally Narcissus realizes that his would-be lover is just an image—the image of his overblown ego.

Now what to do? Die of heartbreak, of course—which is doubly heartbreaking, since his lover will die with him. As Echo echoes his parting cries of "alas" and "farewell," Narcissus wastes away from his burning passion, leaving only a small white and gold flower—the narcissus—to mark his place. But even death does not spare him vanity's torments: once ushered into the underworld, Narcissus is ensared by his reflection in the river Styx.

Back on earth, Ovid's tale made Narcissus an everlasting emblem of self-love. The English term "narcissism," however, was not coined for this condition until Samuel Taylor Coleridge confessed to it in a letter of 1822. Later in the century, the British psychologist Havelock Ellis invoked the myth in describing the "perversion" of autoeroticism, which led to the adoption of "narcissism" as a pejorative psychoanalytic term, whence it filtered into popular usage.

As for the flower Narcissus left in his wake, it takes its name not from the mythical lover-boy but from the Greek *narko*, "numbness," referring to the effect of eating its flower. From *narko* also stem numerous other English terms, such as "narcolepsy," "narcotic," and, from the latter, the slang expression "narc."

EROTIC

Though the ancient Greeks sometimes seem pretty strange, in many ways they were just like us. They were, for example, scared to death of love, or at least of physical desire, which they called *eros*. In Homer's poems, *eros* is a blinding and confusing force superior to gods and men alike, driving them willy-nilly into lovers' arms. For Hesiod, Eros is an immortal being, older than the Titans, who is both a great creating force and the god who "loosens the limbs and damages the mind."

So Eros was originally an emotional terrorist, inflicting strange, uncontrollable feelings and inspiring endless cruelties. But the lyric poets and philosophers of later centuries would emphasize Eros's creative powers, eventually coming to view him as downright playful, even cute. A very old god in Hesiod, Eros would age in reverse, growing younger in the art of each passing century. By the fourth century B.C., the Greeks imagined him as a child-god, son of Aphrodite, who delighted in practical jokes and made a point of outwitting anyone who mocked his power.

Eros (Cupid to the Romans) was also a bit spoiled and inclined to tantrums, and his fits made even the gods quail (he was known on occasion to break Zeus's thunderbolts into little bitty pieces). His principal instruments of vengeance, first mentioned by the Greek dramatist Euripides, were his arrows of gold and lead. The golden arrows would inflame their target's passions, sometimes resulting in happiness and sometimes in disaster [*see* AN ECHO AND NARCISSISM, p. 55]. The leaden arrows, however, were just plain bad, since they inspired only disgust and hatred. You may have noticed that Cupid tends to shoot these arrows in tandem: as soon as you're hit by a golden one, he aims a leaden arrow at the object of your fancy.

This is why the poet Sappho called Eros "bitter-sweet," and the reason that the "Erotic passion," according to Walter Charelton, "is allowed by all learned men to be a species of Melancholy." Charelton was the first (in 1651) to use the word "erotic" in English, though the now-obsolete equivalent "erotical" had appeared a generation earlier. It would be a few more centuries, however, before a word was coined for the more punishing effects of Eros's power—namely "erotomania," first defined by William Van Buren and Edward Keyes in 1874 as "a species of insanity." The old god of ancient Greece may have grown younger and cuter, but he's still apt to damage the mind.

FLORA AND FAUNA

"Flora and fauna" is more than a fancy way of saying "plants and animals"; it's virtually a divine invocation. To the Romans, Flora and Faunus were nature gods who, as you might have guessed, nurtured and protected flora and fauna, respectively.

Of the two, Faunus (sometimes identified with Pan) enjoyed the more interesting festivals, called Lupercalia after one of his epithets, which is believed to derive from the Greek for "averter of wolves." At these Lupercalia, held on February 15, two goats and a dog would be sacrificed and their skins fashioned into whips. Two of Rome's more athletic young men (once including Marc Antony), naked save for simple loincloths, would then take these whips and run through the streets, thrashing everyone in range. Incredibly, such whippings were supposed to bring the victims luck; women in particular welcomed the lash, which they believed a remedy for infertility.

Flora's festivals, called Floralia, were altogether more sedate, though they came to feature somewhat indecent farcical productions. Perhaps these lewd episodes were due to Greek influence, but Christian writers of late antiquity circulated the story that Flora was actually a courtesan in early Rome who bequeathed her substantial earnings to the city, thus meriting honorary godhood. This tale is absurd—the goddess Flora is older than Rome itself—though it is true that a certain prostitute named Flora did achieve fame and fortune as the lover of Pompey the Great.

The modern senses of "flora" and "fauna" both date to the eighteenth century, though they were not originally used together. Much older is the word "faun," which was first used by Chaucer and which refers to rowdy satyr-like spirits thought to be adherents of Faunus. In more recent times "faun" has served as the male version of "nymph," though the connotations are less pejorative. Nabokov, however, did suggest "faunlet" as the complement to "nymphet" when like connotations are desired [*see* A NYMPH, p. 75].

A GENIUS

It's a good thing the Mensa Society didn't have a chapter in ancient Rome, because there's no way it could have kept its cherished exclusivity. Which is to say that there were a great many geniuses back then; in fact, while no man was one, every man had one.

The solution to this riddle is simple once you know that the Latin *genius* meant "generative power" or "vital principal" (from *genare*, "to beget, to generate"). A man's genius was a spirit born with him and entrusted with his care—in other words, his guardian angel. (Women were also born with such a spirit, called a *iuno* after the goddess Juno.) The *genius* of the eldest male in the family also served as the household's collective *genius*, and the idea of "the genius of a place," or *genius loci*, was later extended to all localities, whether or not anyone lived there.

Originally thought of, like the Greek *daimon* [*see* A DEMON, p. 53], as an external guardian spirit, the *genius* was gradually internalized, so that it came to stand for a person's character and desires, and eventually for what we would call his soul. From this latter sense is derived the English word "genius," which originally signified "the essence of one's character" and "natural aptitude." The modern concept of genius, as extraordinary native talent, did not develop until the late eighteenth century, at the time of the Romantic movement. Already disposed to exalt poets and artists, the Romantics attributed their special powers to nature rather than to skill, and, in Germany especially, this power was sometimes equated with divine inspiration.

Curiously enough, the Latin *genius* also became identified in the sixteenth century with the Arabic *jinn*, a word found in the *Arabian Nights* which refers to spirits who meddle in human affairs. The Latin *genius*, by way of its plural *genii*, eventually yielded in this connection to the form "genie." So, ironically, the English word that comes closest to meaning what the Romans originally meant by *genius* is actually more directly related to an Arabic term than to its Latin original.

A HERMAPHRODITE

Like many myths, that of Hermaphroditus seems to be an elaborate rationalization of rituals whose original motives had grown obscure. It is possible, for example, that during marriage ceremonies in certain parts of the ancient Near East men and women would exchange clothing, perhaps to signify a mingling of the sexes. This practice may account for the rather bizarre representations, found on the island of Cyprus, of the love-goddess Aphrodite sporting a beard. Hermes, as a fertility god likewise invoked in marriage rituals, was sometimes depicted with a woman's breasts.

Such ambiguities did not sit well with the Greeks, who preferred their gods well-defined sexually. So eventually there arose a story to explain away these anomalies, involving a liaison between Hermes and Aphrodite. From their union Aphrodite bore a child named, appropriately enough, Hermaphroditus, and he was a handsome young tyke. Handsome, but not well-versed in the affairs of the heart. At about age fifteen Hermaphroditus happened upon a beautiful Asian lake (in some accounts a fountain) and its presiding water-nymph, Salmacis. When the nymph glimpsed Hermaphroditus it was love at first sight; all her powers of seduction, however, came to naught.

But Salmacis was not beaten. She hid in the bushes, keeping her eye on Hermaphroditus. As she had expected, the boy was so enchanted by the lake's beauty that he decided to take a dip. Once in the water, however, he was in Salmacis's domain, so as she slipped in and grabbed him he was powerless to resist. Holding Hermaphroditus tight, Salmacis prayed fervently that their two bodies would never again be separated.

The gods heard this prayer and took it at face value. Slowly, the nymph's body merged with the boy's until they were one; Hermaphroditus emerged both man and woman. As you might guess, he was less than thrilled, and in his turn prayed that the gods would curse the lake so that any man who bathed in it would lose his masculinity. And so it came to pass—or at least, so became the local superstition, which persisted well into the early first century A.D.

It was only natural that persons or animals endowed with traits of both sexes would come to be called "hermaphrodites," once Englishmen (in the fourteenth century) coined a word for the condition. Over time the term was generalized to include plants and lower animals which contained in themselves both of the halves necessary for reproduction— thistles and earthworms, for example. But by then the word had already assumed negative connotations, mostly by way of its use as a label for an effeminate man or virile woman, or for an unnatural or pernicious combination. Thomas Hobbes, for example, referred in 1651 to "Hermaphrodite opinions of [certain] moral philosophers, partly right and comely, partly brutal and wild."

HYPNOSIS AND MORPHINE

Hypnotism was not widely practiced before the early nineteenth century, when it was popularized by the Austrian crank F. A. Mesmer. (Mesmer, after whom the technique was also called "mesmerism," thought the hypnotist charmed his patient with "animal magnetism.") But the Greeks knew about Hypnos, if not hypnotism, thousands of years before Mesmer.

As Hesiod explains, Hypnos, whose name means "sleep," was a son of Nyx (Night) who lived in the underworld and, unlike his brother Thanatos (Death), shunned the light of day. By definition a rather boring god whose only job is to pour a sleeping potion from a horn onto the brows of the weary, Hypnos lacks exciting myths, though he does make a cameo appearance in Homer's *Iliad*.

Ovid does his best to make Sleep interesting, but his tale is not really worth repeating here. Suffice it to say that Sleep

(*Somnus* in Latin) is given a son named Morpheus, whose name Ovid invented from the Greek *morphai*, "form" or "shape." Morpheus is a god of dreams, a shape-shifter and mimic who penetrates the sleeping mind, impersonating human forms and speech. (He works in tandem with his brothers Ikelos, who imitates beasts, and Phantasos, who represents inanimate objects.)

The association of Hypnos with hypnotism is obvious enough—in fact, the English word "hypnotic" originally meant "sleep-inducing" and referred to soporific drugs. But what morphine has to do with its namesake Morpheus isn't as clear. What seems to have happened is that medieval and Renaissance poets—among them Chaucer and Spenser—confused Morpheus with his father Somnus, taking the former as the god of sleep rather than of dreams. Thus when an opium derivative was discovered to kill pain and ease the suffering to sleep, it was poetically, though incorrectly, named after Morpheus.

The ancient Greeks wouldn't have known what to make of all this, since they had no god Morpheus to begin with. Their word *morphai*, however, which Ovid appropriated to name his character, is the direct source for such words as "metamorphosis" (change of form), "polymorphous" (taking many shapes), and "morphology" (the study of biological or grammatical forms). Where sleep is concerned, though, the Greek *hypnos* and the Latin *somnus* (source of "somnolent") are the more proper roots. If Chaucer hadn't been dozing off while reading his Ovid, we might more correctly be calling morphine "somnine" or "hypnine"—tongue-twisters that make the mistake sound downright elegant.

LETHAL AND LETHARGIC

"Lethal" and "lethargic," though unlikely cousins, both derive from the Greek word *lethe*, "oblivion." As with other merely human powers and afflictions, the Greeks lent *lethe* a mythical personification, in fact two of them. One, a child of Eris (Discord), has appropriately enough sunk into literary oblivion. But the other, an infernal stream and the source of forgetfulness, is better remembered.

According to the Greeks, this Lethe was one of five underworld rivers, though somewhat removed from the other four. After crossing the Styx, shades of the dead were forced to drink from Lethe to cleanse themselves of earthly memories. Philosophers of reincarnation claimed that shades also drank from the river before being shuttled back up to this vale of tears for another shot at a virtuous life.

Our word "lethargy" stems directly from *lethargia*, an ancient Greek medical term, after the river, for a disease that induced intense drowsiness or prolonged sleep. Medieval Englishmen borrowed this term, through Latin, for the disease, but at about the same time began using it to mean "torpor," "apathy," and "laziness" as well.

The Romans, figuring that the point of the Greek myth was that utter oblivion was the same thing as being dead, coined the words *lethum* (death) and *lethalis* (deadly). Our word "lethal" derives from the latter and was first used (circa 1583) in the phrase "lethal sin," i.e., mortal sin. The word came to mean "deadly" in the literal sense by the early seventeenth century.

THE MUSES

MUSIC · MUSEUM · CALLIOPE · TO MUSE

"Sing, goddess, the anger of Peleus's son Achilles": so begins Homer's *Iliad*. The poet does not name this goddess, but we know that she is one of the Muses, daughters of Zeus by the Titan Mnemosyne (Memory) and inspirers of all artistic endeavor.

By the time the last book of Homer's *Odyssey* was written down, the Greeks had decided there were nine of these Muses. Hesiod was the first to name them: Calliope, Clio, Erato, Euterpe, Melpomene, Polyhymnia, Terpsichore, Thalia, and Urania. In general, these names refer to various modes of expression, but in Hesiod the different Muses don't really have distinct attributes; all we are told is that Calliope ("She of the Beautiful Voice") is their ringleader and that they collectively inspire kings and poets with wisdom and eloquence.

If you had to be a mythological figure, you could do a lot worse than a Muse. These nymphs (later promoted to minor goddesses) spent their days singing and dancing around the sacred springs of Mount Helicon and Mount Parnassus (both in central Greece). Their workweek was short and pretty painless; they merely had to serenade the gods as they ate. The Muses were thus the first dinner-club entertainers. Once in a while a poet would invoke one or more of them to get an epic going; and while there was no overtime pay the Muses were usually awarded top billing.

Anyone who challenged the Muses' supremacy in dancing and singing was promptly and soundly defeated in contest, and always punished for the presumption. This is how the Sirens lost their wings, and it's also how the haughty Pierides got theirs—when the victorious Muses turned them into birds [see PEGASUS, p. 162]. Their vocal talents and a growing reputation as inspirers of wisdom earned the Muses numerous cults throughout Greece, and several important philosophical schools—Plato's Academy and Aristotle's Lyceum, for example—began as Muse-cults.

As a result, the word *Mouseion*, originally "a temple or haunt of the Muses," came to mean "a place of research and learning." In ancient times, the most famous such *Mouseion*—"museum" in English—was established circa 280 B.C. by Ptolemy I at Alexandria. Known simply as The Museum, it soon became the world's preeminent research institution and library, with some 100 scholars in residence and catered refreshments. You might think of The Museum as the first think tank.

A practitioner of the Muses' arts—whether bard, dancer, or scholar—was called a *mousikos*, and the art itself called *mousike*. These were once upon a time rather general terms, but since the Muses' principal talent was singing, and since the Greeks considered song the highest art, *mousike* came to refer in particular to the making of pleasing sounds—in other words, to "music," an English descendent of the Greek *mousike*.

Though musicians all, the Muses later, in the days of the Roman Empire, took on more specific functions. Historians, for example, looked to Clio for patronage, while comedians turned to Thalia, tragedians to Melpomene, epic poets to Calliope, lyric poets to Euterpe, erotic poets to Erato, dancers to Terpsichore, hymnodists to Polyhymnia, and astronomers to Urania. (Astronomy may seem out of place in this list, but at one time the arts were thought of as sciences and the sciences as arts.) This is why you might, in a pedantic mood, call a dancer a "terpsichorean," and why the application of quantitative analysis to history is known as "cliometrics."

Joshua C. Stoddard of Massachusetts must have thought he had an epic invention on his hands when, in 1855, he devised a steam-whistle organ and called it the "calliope." Others have begged to differ, and one must agree that the

Greeks would never have called its namesake "beautiful-voiced" if she sounded like Stoddard's contraption. Shrill banks of some dozen to twenty whistles, calliopes once could be heard miles away as they piped out standard marches and dance tunes from the decks of American showboats or from the fringes of traveling circuses. In one of the earliest written references to the new instrument, Sir William Howard Russell spoke, in 1863, for many tender-eared victims: "The whistle sounds, and the calliope shrieks out 'Dixie' incessantly."

Surprisingly, while affected coinages like "terpsichorean" and "cliometrics" do trace back to the muses, the simple verb "to muse" does not. Rather, and rather bizarrely, it ultimately derives from the medieval Latin *mus*, "snout" (whence also the word "muzzle"). From *mus* arose the Italian verb *musare*, "to hold one's snout in the air," as dogs do when uncertain of a scent; this being the canine equivalent of meditation, the verb eventually took on the meaning "to reflect," "to speculate"—a sense most likely influenced by the pun on the Greek Muses. The secondary meanings "trifle," "dally" also arise from the Italian *musare*, based on a less charitable view of dogs' ability to muse.

A NEMESIS

The Greek gods were nothing if not jealous, especially of uppity mortals. Whenever someone started thinking himself too happy or too powerful, the gods would unleash their agent Nemesis, a personification of the dictum that "the higher you climb, the harder you fall."

Nemesis, according to Hesiod a comely daughter of the goddess Nyx, eventually caught Zeus's eye but hoped to evade his pursuit by taking on a series of disguises. Zeus, however, could not be so easily fooled, and in the guise of a swan he finally caught up with Nemesis, who at the time was posing as a goose.

Zeus, an ironic fellow, decided that since Nemesis had thought herself trickier than the supreme god, he would assign her the task of cutting pretentious mortals down to size. As a sideline Nemesis also boosted those who fell too far, and by thus balancing the scales she preserved the cosmic equilibrium.

Of all the Greek gods imported by the Romans, Nemesis proved among the most useful. Before embarking on any war, the Romans would make sacrifices to the goddess and proclaim her their partisan, thus seeking to convince the world (if not themselves) that their aggressions were just. To drive the point home, they built a statue of Nemesis on the Capitoline, their seat of government.

All the earliest English references to "Nemesis" (invariably capitalized) are either to the Greek goddess or to the abstraction she personifies, namely just retribution. Those meanings now more common—"dogged foe" and "source of injury"—are twentieth-century inventions, typically lacking the moral content of the Greek original. While it is now permissible to say such things as "junk food is my nemesis" and to apply the term to any old enemy, one's just deserts are rarely an issue.

A Nymph

"Nymph" is not the most flattering thing you might call the modern young woman—especially since it's become shorthand for the more negative derivatives "nymphet" and "nymphomaniac." This is an unfortunate case of guilt by association, since "nymph," in its pure form meaning simply "a beautiful young lady," ultimately derives from the name that ancient Greeks gave to very delightful and generally benevolent spirits, the most innocent of mythical creatures.

These nymphs, daughters of Zeus, were local nature spirits, beautiful maidens of the mountains, forests, and springs, given to dancing and poetry. They were not, however, immortal, though they usually lived as long as the natural objects whose vitality they embodied (not necessarily a long time if you were the nymph of a particular tree). The nymphs were also said to have curative and prophetic powers, though these often came with strings attached. And while nymphs were credited when nature behaved well, they were blamed when it behaved badly; though generally admired, they were thus also considered somewhat dangerous.

A few of these nymphs proved particularly troublesome—Calypso, for example, an island spirit and the daughter of Atlas, who detained the hero Odysseus for eight years. Nymphs were more often the victim, though, as is proved by the numerous stories of gods attempting to force their will upon them. Even if a nymph resisted, she was liable to end up as a tree or a patch of reeds [see A SYRINGE, p. 84].

And now the ultimate insult: their name has been turned into one. For hundreds of years "nymph" was used as a metaphor for an innocently beautiful girl; that was before William Cullen coined "nymphomania" in his treatise *Nosology*, published in English in 1800. The term was somewhat technical (referring to a supposed medical condition), but that fault would be corrected in this century. Gradually, following simplistic interpretations of what Vladimir Nabokov meant by the term in his 1955 novel *Lolita*, "nymphet" succumbed to the corrosion of innuendo, closely followed by "nymph" itself. (Ironic, given the Greek nymphs' strenuous efforts to shield their virtue.) Maybe people should pick on somebody their own size (and sex), like Pan.

A PANACEA

"Panacea" means in English exactly what it meant in Greek: "cure-all." While today nobody uses the word without contempt—as a sneer at some bogus solution to a big problem—the Greeks not only believed in cure-alls, they went so far as to name a goddess after them.

The mythical Panacea was a daughter of the Greek medicine-god Asclepius (son of Apollo); and like her siblings, she personified one of her father's powers: the ability to heal with plants. The Romans later applied Panacea's name to a particular genus of herbs they fancied could heal all diseases. Following the lead of the natural historian Pliny the Elder, English writers, using the term "Panace," identified these magical herbs with a series of real plants—a new one, in fact, every time the last proved ineffective.

The more faithful spelling "panacea" arrived to English slightly later, in a 1548 translation of Erasmus's commentary on the Gospel according to Luke, where it is defined as a medicine "effectual and of much virtue, but known to no man." This idea was already being laughed at by the end of the century, though it would continue to be advanced until at least the mid-1700s. But of course, while the notion of an herbal cure-all has gone the way of phrenology, ideological panaceas continue to flourish. And some among us will agree with one character in Mrs. Henry Wood's 1867 novel *Orville College* that coffee is indeed a "panacea for most ailments."

TO PANIC

The noun "panic"—originally and more properly "panic fear"—stems from the Latin adjective *Panica*, meaning "related to or inspired by Pan," the Greek god of herds. Pan seems to have come to Greece by way of Egypt, where he was an old and powerful fertility god represented in ritual and art as a goat. Taking this symbolism a bit literally, the Greeks imagined Pan as a goat with the upper body of a man, hairy, horned, lustful, and, for some reason, perpetually flushed—perhaps a detail related to his amorous inclination.

In any case, Greek herdsmen would attribute whatever happened to their flocks, good or bad, to Pan. This included the sudden terror which would often seize a herd *en masse*, from which arose the tale that Pan could with one cry send groups of animals or men into what was accordingly called a

"panic fear." (Thus "panic" is still more properly used of a crowd than of an individual.)

Since Pan was supposed to haunt forests and mountainsides, anything that went bump in the night in such places was supposedly the god himself. While vacationing from scaring innocent Greeks, Pan would occasionally lend a hand to nobler causes. For example, he helped Zeus rout the Giants [see TITANIC, p. 6] by sending them into a panic, and he performed similar services for the Athenians in their war against Persia in the early fifth century B.C.

Why Pan is named Pan is a question which perplexed many a Greek, especially since the name differs from the Greek word *pan*, "all," only by an accent. Perhaps it's because his peculiar appearance and lustiness delighted "all" the gods. Or perhaps, as some claimed, it is because he was the son of Queen Penelope of Ithaca (Odysseus's wife) by "all" the suitors who pestered her during her husband's absence. (Less absurd accounts make Hermes the father.) Or maybe the Pan/*pan* pun is really only a pun; the god's name may be more directly related to the Greek for "one who feeds," since he helped feed and nurture the herds.

As Rich as Plutus

He's everybody's favorite deity, but few know his name—he's Plutus, god of wealth. This antic fellow sprang from a nectar-inflamed union of Demeter, goddess of growth and harvests, with the young Titan Iasion. At first Plutus, as the god of bountiful crops, merely personified one aspect of his mother's power. But as Greek society grew more commercial, a good harvest became equated with riches in general.

Plutus was also linked by name to Pluto (a.k.a. Hades), lord of the underworld. Wealth may seem to have little to do with death, but the Greeks understood the connection between decay and fertility. In contrast to this inexorable cycle, however, Plutus's bounty seemed to accrue arbitrarily. Thus the god was represented as blind, lame, and winged: blind, as he paid little care to merit; lame, as he took his time arriving; and winged, as he vanished more quickly than he came.

Plutus has lent his name to a few English words and phrases. The Romans, observing that the wealthy are often moral cowards, were fond of the expression *timidus Plutus*, "as fearful as Plutus," which became an English catchphrase by the seventeenth century. More common today is the simpler "as rich as Plutus," which seems to be modeled on the earlier proverb "as rich as Croesus."

From the root meaning of Plutus's name, we also derive "plutocracy" (rule by the wealthiest) and "plutocrat." Less familiar, though more amusing, are such coinages as "plutolatry" (by analogy with "idolatry," the worship of filthy lucre) and "plutomania," the delusion that one is immensely wealthy. In our language as in society, Plutus is everywhere.

PROTEAN

"Protean," meaning "shape-shifting" or "variable," refers to the mythical Greek figure Proteus, a talented impersonator who seems to have shifted shape every time someone wrote about him. To Homer, Proteus was a spirit who served the sea-god Poseidon; to Hesiod, he was a minor god who guided herds of sea mammals; to Herodotus, Euripides, and others he was an Egyptian king.

Homer's tale is hardly the most credible, but it proved the most influential. In the *Odyssey*, the Greek hero Menelaus, Sparta's king and Helen's husband, relates his visit to immortal Proteus, "the Old Man of the Sea," on the Egyptian island Pharos (later site of the famous lighthouse). Proteus, endowed by Poseidon with soothsaying powers, would emerge from the sea only once a day, at noon, to nap on the shore. If any mortal could then seize him, the old man would answer his questions. But Proteus, who had the power to assume any form whatsoever—frightful tiger, scorching fire, whirlwind, river, or what have you—could not be easily caught. (Menelaus succeeded, but that's another story.)

The Greek historian Herodotus, unable to swallow this business whole, still figured there must have been some connection between Menelaus and Proteus. He preferred the following tale, as told to him by Egyptian priests:

When the Trojan prince Paris paid a visit to Menelaus, he was so enchanted by Queen Helen that he outraged his host by seducing her and then quickly taking her off by sea. Paris and his convoy, however, were blown off course and stranded

on the Egyptian coast. The good Egyptian king Proteus heard of this and brought Paris to Memphis for questioning.

Paris, not much known for his courage, carefully avoided the truth, which sent Proteus into a rage. Though the king suppressed the urge to execute the Trojan, even agreeing to let him go, he refused to allow Paris to take Helen or her wealth with him. Meanwhile the Greeks, ignorant of these events, had decided to wage war with Troy over Paris's crime; they merely scoffed at the Trojans' claim that Helen was dallying in Memphis.

Herodotus does believe them—why, he rightly wonders, wouldn't the Trojans unload a kept woman if that would put an end to the Greeks' punishing assault? Eventually the Greeks ask the same question, and Menelaus decides to visit Proteus just in case. Finding his wife in Memphis, Menelaus rejoices, avails himself of Proteus's hospitality for a few days, and then sets off with Helen for Sparta. But Menelaus proves an ingrate; when storms prevent his passage home, he returns to the coast and sacrifices two Egyptian infants to the gods. Thus ends the friendship between Egypt and Sparta.

In one fell swoop, Herodotus manages to substitute a relatively credible historical account for the older fictions of Proteus and Paris [see AN APPLE OF DISCORD, p. 178]. But history doesn't always conquer fantasy; even those, such as Euripides, who basically accepted Herodotus's version of events felt compelled to reintegrate details from Homer's, which would remain by far the more popular.

In English, the sea-god first appears in *The Romance of the Rose* (ca. 1400), where he's described as one "that could him change/ In every shape, homely [familiar] and strange." By the late sixteenth century, Proteus's name had become a metaphor describing someone capable of taking on different shapes or disguises—a stage actor, for example. Out of this usage soon arose the adjective "protean," which is still in use though "Proteus" itself is not. This passage from noun to adjective was the god's final metamorphosis.

A SYRINGE

The frisky goat-god Pan chased his share of nymphs, but he had a particular crush on Syrinx, an Arcadian water-spirit. As a devotee of the chaste goddess Artemis, however, Syrinx wanted nothing to do with her hairy pursuer. The patented mythical chase scene ensued, with Pan eventually cornering the nymph on the banks of the river Ladon.

Desperate, Syrinx begged her sisters to change her into something nondescript—a clump of marsh reeds, for example. Presto changeo: as soon as Pan was upon her, Syrinx was transformed, and the god came up with an armful of reeds rather than an armful of nymph.

But Pan's desire did not cool, and he resolved to keep Syrinx by his side forever. Hearing the wind evoke a plaintive sigh from the reeds, he hit on the idea of waxing together a row of them, cut to different sizes, which he could pipe on whenever he was lonely or bored. This pipe was called a *syrinx* in Greek and became a trendy accessory among the local shepherds.

More generally, *syrinx* came to refer to anything pipe-shaped, such as one's spear case or the tubes Greeks used to shoot spitballs. This word very likely yielded the medieval Latin term *siringa*, and thus the fifteenth-century English word "siryng," referring to a tube fitted like the modern eyedropper with a bladder at one end. Though this device proved most useful to doctors, it came in handy around the house, too, and the word was very broadly applied to any tube used to suck up or squirt liquids. After the hypodermic syringe was invented in the nineteenth century, however, the

term gradually came to refer particularly to that wicked instrument.

A TERMINUS

TERMINAL · TERM · TERMINOLOGY

Terminus, as the Roman god of boundary stones, was a sort of lesser Janus [*see* p. 12]; but lesser or greater he demanded showy rituals. Besides throwing special parties, called Terminalia, each February in his honor, the Romans would often duly make sacrifices to Terminus at their nearby boundary stone, pouring ashes and blood into a trench, covering it with pine branches, and then setting the contents on fire. When the show was over, they would set the stone on top of the trench and go back home hopeful that their neighborhood was safe from evil influences.

Over time, both statues of Terminus—generally just rude stones, sometimes with human heads—and then all boundary markers came to be called *termini*, and by association *terminus* also came to mean "end-point." Obviously, the English words "terminus" and "terminal" derive from the Latin, but so, surprisingly, does the word "term," whose root meaning is preserved when we speak of a pregnancy "coming to term." Originally used to mean "limit" or "end," "term" later came to signify "a limited period of time" and then "the limiting conditions of an agreement or duty." Thus we speak of "an academic term" and "negotiating terms."

The use of "term" to mean "a verbal or mathematical expression" is due largely to the Greek mathematician Euclid. Euclid used the Greek word for "boundary point" to speak of arithmetic variables, which he considered the "terms" or limits of larger sets or quantities. Thus in English "term" came to be used as the name for an element in a mathematical ratio, first in 1542 by Robert Recorde, who said that "You call the Numerator and Denominator the Terms of the Fraction."

Meanwhile, back in the classical period, Latin logicians extended the use of *terminus* from mathematics to philosophical argument, applying it to the definition or limitation of a concept and by extension to precisely defined and fixed expressions—thus our word "terminology." In English this philosophical usage of "term" preceded the mathematical sense, showing up by the fourteenth century. It also well predates the expression "term-trotter," coined in 1607 for aspiring barristers who trotted off to London's courts for the law term.

THE WHEEL OF FORTUNE

The Romans had *vanni* (fans), and they wagered against the Wheel of Fortune, but so far as I know they had no equivalent of Vanna White. Had they known what they were missing they probably would have blamed the goddess Fortuna (luck personified), who spun the wheel in Vanna's stead.

No sooner would Fortuna bestow wealth or fame than she would contrive to wipe it out with disaster or disgrace. Such giddy flip-flops reminded the ancients of the turning of a great wheel—a Ferris wheel on a cosmic scale. Thus Fortuna was often depicted as grasping a wheel or sometimes, because she was fancied to influence all earthly endeavors, holding a globe. She clearly had a thing for round objects.

Fortuna's wheel has always been her most famous toy. In fact, the first time the word "fortune" appears in English, in a lame pun dating to about 1300, so does Fortune's wheel: "Dame fortune turns then her wheel/ And casts us down into a well." Sooner or later, someone was bound to realize that "Wheel of Fortune" would be a clever name for a lottery wheel, a seventeenth-century invention in which lottery slips were mixed. That someone was an anonymous rhyming moralist, writing in a 1763 issue of *British Magazine*: "Beware the Wheel of Fortune—'tis a gin [trap],/ You'll lose a dozen times for once you win." Well, no kidding—but isn't that the game's attraction?

The modern wheel of fortune bears little resemblance to the old lottery wheel, except that both are round; it's more like an upright roulette wheel and is now found mostly at carnivals. As for the televised version, a glorified hybrid of roulette and hangman, many would claim that Vanna, rather than the thrill of victory, is the real attraction. In any case, the game betrays its namesake goddess, since while chance may determine the dollar value of any guess, whether that guess is correct has as much to do with skill, to use the word loosely, as with luck.

HEROES,
HEROINES,
AND ANTIHEROES

AN ACHILLES' HEEL

While Achilles' heel is now his best-known feature, Homer doesn't breathe a word of it in the *Iliad*, Achilles' star vehicle. If Homer's hero has a problem, it's his pride, which is indeed of epic proportions. In later Greek accounts, Achilles has a weak spot for the Trojan princess Polyxena, but no weak spot on his heel. It took the Romans to invent this detail, which is suggested by Ovid but made explicit only in Statius's *Achilleid*, a minor epic of the first century A.D.

According to Statius, Achilles' mother, Thetis, a sea-nymph, thought her son perfect except for one unbearable defect: he was mortal. So one day she gathered the little hero in her arms and made off for the banks of the river Styx [*see* p. 199], dunking Achilles a few times in the poisoned waters to render his skin invulnerable to wounds. But since Thetis wasn't about to throw her son into the Styx, by any reckoning a very nasty body of water, one small spot on his body had to remain dry—and this, of course, was his heel.

So in an attempt to fix one defect, Thetis left Achilles with another. And once his enemies found out about it, he was as good as dead—especially since those enemies were Poseidon and Apollo. Achilles had grown up to be quite an annoyance to the Trojans, whom the divine duo favored in the Trojan War. After the Greek had spoiled one too many of their well-laid plans, these gods directed the cowardly Trojan prince Paris to shoot a poisoned arrow at Achilles' heel while he wasn't looking. So the fate Thetis had hoped to avoid came to pass anyway, as fates tend to do.

It would take another eighteen centuries, however, for Englishmen to coin the phrase "Achilles' heel." Samuel Taylor Coleridge approximates it in *The Friend* (1810), where Ireland is described as "that vulnerable heel of the British Achilles"; but the phrase as we know it traces only to 1864 and Thomas Carlyle. In addition to begetting this metaphor for a person's fatal flaw or most vulnerable point, the legend also inspired the slightly more literal medical term *tendo Achillis*, or "Achilles' tendon." If you don't know where your Achilles' tendon is, just pull it some time and you'll never forget.

AN ADONIS

Picture an adonis, and you're likely to envision one of those tanned, brawny specimens on Muscle Beach. But according to Ovid, the original Adonis, so good looking as to be almost effeminate, never lived long enough to grow a proper muscle.

Adonis, in other words, was merely a boy, and a spoiled one at that, which makes it doubly strange that the love-goddess Venus would fall madly in love with him. But it's not really her fault; while smooching it up with her son Cupid, she accidently sat on one of his arrows, and Adonis just happened to be the first animate object to come along.

That's how Ovid explains things, but he didn't invent the basic story, which has roots in Syrian legends predating even the earliest Greek literature. (Adonis's name derives from the Semitic *adon,* "lord.") And "roots" is precisely the word, since Adonis was born out of a myrrh tree [*see* p. 124] and was fated to wind up as a plant. Not only was Adonis girlish, he was also something of a nature boy.

Since Adonis's mother is now a tree, Venus plays parent as well as lover, and she gets to be, in Adonis's view, annoyingly protective. The one thing that thrills him is hunting, which he pursues with a reckless passion; Venus, rightly fearful, repeatedly warns him to avoid beasts capable of defending themselves—boar, for example. Of course, the petulant Adonis is only spurred on by her warnings, and one dark day an angry boar gores him in a delicate place. (In some versions, the boar is loosed on Adonis by the vengeful goddess Diana, Venus's rival. In others, the boar is actually Venus's jealous lover Mars in disguise.)

Whoever was responsible for Adonis's death—if the fault wasn't his own—Venus was mortified. When she found his body, she wept tears and poured nectar on the spot, causing his blood to bring forth a brand new flower, called the anemone, from the Greek for "wind-flower." Just as the wind steals the anemone's frail young petals, Adonis was cut off in the flower of youth.

As far as Ovid is concerned, that's the end of the story. But according to older myths, Adonis never dies once and for all, but rather descends to the underworld each winter and rises to earth again in the spring. This cycle of death and rebirth is due to the ancient fancy that Adonis was a vegetation god, a fancy common to Phoenicia and Egypt as well as Greece.

The poetical version, however, won out over the naked myth, and it was the version familiar in Shakespeare's day, when Ovid was all the rage. But while the tale itself was commonplace, "adonis" itself wasn't used as a common noun before the late eighteenth century, and then mostly with tongue in cheek. Before this century, in fact, an "adonis" was a dandy, if he was a man; otherwise, it was a particular kind of men's wig.

AN AMAZON

One of the most curious Greek legends concerns a race of warlike superwomen known as Amazons, who by most accounts lived on the coast of the Black Sea in what is now north central Turkey. You might think of the Amazons as the first feminist separatists, since they wanted nothing to do with men, or other women for that matter. But, in the interest of propagation, they would occasionally bite the bullet and venture forth into nearby settlements. Once the local males had satisfied the Amazons' needs, the women would head back home and await the results.

If the results were bad—that is, male—the infant was returned to his father (or, according to some historians, strangled). Girls, on the other hand, were raised according to a strict and demanding regimen and instilled with the proper attitudes. At the appropriate age, each girl's right breast was burnt off so that it would not get in the way as she handled a bow or javelin—thus the name "Amazon," supposedly from the Greek *a-mazos*, "lacking a breast." (Etymologists doubt the derivation, preferring to think that "Amazon" is based on an unidentifiable foreign name.)

As you may well imagine, the Amazons weren't softies, and they caused a good deal of trouble for many legendary heroes—Achilles, Hercules, and Theseus, to name a few. Ancient tales of the Amazons' ferocity led Englishmen to use "amazon" as a metaphorical term for any warlike, muscular, or assertive woman. A few insect species also profited by the comparison: in his amusingly titled *The Feminine Monarchy*;

or, A *Treatise Concerning Bees* (1609), Charles Butler makes reference to "Amazonian dames" (queen bees) who sooner or later "begin to wax weary of their mates," with gruesome results. Three centuries later, a species of red ant was dubbed the "Amazon ant" because the neuters made a practice of kidnapping and enslaving youngsters of other ant species.

BY JOVE!

A CASSANDRA

The only thing worse than a pessimist is one who is always right—meet Cassandra, a legendary Trojan princess. As the story goes, even in the hubbub of the war with Greece Cassandra's beauty brought her to the attention of the god Apollo, a Trojan partisan, who offered her prophetic powers if she would gratify his passions. Cassandra agreed to the deal, but, once Apollo had done his part, she reneged on hers. The angry god put a curse on her, ensuring that while she could predict the future, nobody would ever believe her.

In fact, not only was Cassandra ignored, but everyone thought her a raving lunatic. And then things got even worse. First, Achilles slew her brother Hector and the Greeks burned Troy to the ground, despite her prophecies on both counts. Then, after being raped by the Greek bully Ajax, she was carted off to Mycenae by King Agamemnon, the victors' commander. No sooner had they arrived than Cassandra began ranting about Queen Clytaemnestra's plot to have her husband killed; once again, she was ignored, and so both she and Agamemnon bit the dust.

Thus Cassandra is not a role model I'd recommend to anyone—not just because her fate was unenviable, but also because there's no fun in being right when nobody's left alive to tell "I told you so." To add insult to injury, those who nowadays bandy about the term "Cassandra" tend to forget the whole point of her story, namely that she *was* prophetic; her name is now just a synonym for "doomsayer" or "wet blanket."

DEUCALION AND THE GREAT FLOOD

The hero Deucalion is sometimes called the "Greek Noah," and with good reason. Deucalion's legend dates at least to the fifth century B.C., and perhaps to the eighth, but in either case it is probably later than the account found in Genesis. Whether or not the Hebrew story directly influenced the Greek, it is certain that the tale of a cataclysmic flood circulated around the Mediterranean in several versions.

As the Greek version goes, Zeus was growing increasingly disgusted with the race of men that had sprung from Pandora and the Titans [see p. 43], so he whisked himself down to earth to make his displeasure known. His first stop was Arcadia, a hotbed of sin ruled at that time by the wicked king Lycaon. Though the Arcadians were suitably awed by the god, Lycaon had grown so arrogant that he virtually laughed in Zeus's face, sinking even so low as to attempt serving the god human flesh for a snack.

This was the last straw. Zeus destroyed Lycaon's family and turned the king himself into a wolf (*lykos* in Greek), and that was just the beginning. Deciding that Lycaon's crimes established once and for all the earthlings' degeneracy, Zeus conjured up a great flood to destroy the entire race. That is, except for two pious Thessalians, Deucalion and his wife, Pyrrha, offspring of Prometheus and Epimetheus, respectively. With Zeus's permission, Prometheus instructed the couple to build an ark, which they boarded just as the waters rose. Nobody, in this version, seems to have considered the poor animals—though Gaia thoughtfully brought forth new ones after the calamity.

Deucalion and Pyrrha eventually landed on the peak of Mount Parnassus. Feeling a little diffident about accomplishing the task all by themselves, they descended the mount to visit an oracle for advice on replenishing their race. In the classic delphic manner, the oracle instructed Deucalion and Pyrrha to toss their grandmother's bones behind them—advice all the more puzzling since their grandmother was the Titans' mother, namely Gaia, the Earth herself.

Putting their heads together, the couple finally deduced that the earth's bones must be stones. Obeying their instructions, they dug up an armful each; the stones Deucalion tossed hit the ground as men, and Pyrrha's as women. They also begat several children the traditional way, including a son named Hellen, who in turn became the great ancestor of the so-called Hellenes, a.k.a. the Greeks.

A great deal of this story of course defies credibility, but it seems likely, given their widespread acceptance in the ancient world, that accounts of the great flood are based on one or more actual events. The Athenian philosopher Xenophon, a student of Socrates, reported that there had been five great floods before the time of the Trojan War, Deucalion's being merely the fourth—not even the worst of them at that. In the Hebrew version there is no doubt that Noah's flood was the first and last of its kind; God in fact promises that such a deluge would never be repeated. Even had Zeus made such a promise, the Greeks would have known better than to believe him.

EUROPE

The Greeks weren't entirely sure where they got the name "Europe," which originally referred to mainland Greece and then (along with "Asia" and "Libya") to one of the three main divisions of the ancient world. The most common view, however, was that continent took its name from Europa, a princess of Tyre in Phoenicia and thus, ironically enough, an Asian.

Europa's story actually has little to do directly with Europe, except that she wound up as queen of Crete. The tale begins when Zeus, the victim once more of Eros's golden arrow, makes his way to Phoenicia, intent on stealing the princess away. To this end he transformed himself into a suave, gentle-looking bull and charmed Europa into mounting his back.

The hot-blooded Zeus then plunged into the sea, leaving the distraught Europa to hang on by a horn. Soon they landed on Crete, where Zeus revealed himself to the maiden, who would in due time bear him two sons, Minos and Rhadamanthus [see THE MINOTAUR, p. 158]. Zeus eventually married Europa off to the Cretan king Asterion, but only redeemed his shameful behavior upon her death, when he elevated her to godhood.

Though by tradition Europa is the continent's namesake (as Asia and Libya are named after more obscure nymphs), the names of both nymph and land mass more likely derive from *Ereb*, Assyrian for "Land of the Setting Sun." Now guess what the Assyrian *Asu* means.

To Fly Too Close to the Sun

If you needed proof that genes aren't infallible, Greek myth offers Daedalus (the smart father) and Icarus (the stupid son). Daedalus, whose name means "artful craftsman," was very clever indeed, a genius (in the modern sense) for invention. Legends say he devised such handy items as the sail, the saw, the folding chair, and glue.

Daedalus was clever, but also jealous. Born and raised in Athens, he was forced into exile after impetuously killing his own nephew Perdix when the latter began showing too much inventive skill. (By one legend, Daedalus threw Perdix into the Aegean, but the boy was revived by the gods as a partridge, which is what *perdix* means in Greek.) Daedalus fled to Crete, where they prized artistry more anyway, and soon ingratiated himself to King Minos with histrionic shows of skill—carving statues, for example, that could walk about and wink.

The problem was that, given a chance to prove his craft, Daedalus didn't discriminate too finely among purposes. On the one hand, he helped Queen Pasiphaë mate with a bull, and then on the other built Minos the Labyrinth to pen up the monstrous result, namely the Minotaur. Then, to finish the job, he gave Princess Ariadne some thread which would prove instrumental in the Minotaur's death. (For more details, *see* p. 158.) Daedalus got away with playing all sides until Minos discovered his treachery, at which point the king threw him into the Labyrinth, tossing in Icarus for good measure.

Unhappily for the Minotaur (who was going to miss lunch) but happily for father and son, Daedalus just happened to have brought along a pile of feathers and some wax, from which he crafted two pairs of wings. He attached one pair to his son's shoulders with a little more wax, and then a pair to his own; in a flash, the two were airborne over the Aegean. Icarus, however—lightheaded, fatheaded, and puffed up with his new power—swooped up through the sky as if to pay a visit to Queen Pasiphaë's father Helios (the Sun). He forgot that wax melts and plunged to his death in the sea near Crete, which then became known as the "Icarian Sea" in honor of his folly.

There was little Daedalus could do, so he continued on his way, eventually landing in Sicily, where he was granted asylum by a local king named Cocalus. When this news reached Crete, an enraged Minos made his way straight to Cocalus's court, demanding the escapee's return. The Sicilian consented, but prevailed upon Minos to let his daughters give him a bath before getting down to business. This bath would prove the Cretan's last. The princesses, in cahoots with Daedalus, doused Minos with hot pitch.

There's no good reason Icarus's demise should be better remembered than Minos's, but there you have it. "To fly too close to the sun" became proverbial, connoting a foolish daring that I suppose is more poetic than mere gullibility. But "to bathe in hot pitch" would also make a nice proverb, apt for those occasions when your undoing is brought on by others' scheming rather than your own delusions. Which do *you* find more flattering?

HALCYON DAYS

Perhaps you thought "halcyon" means "good olde," as in "halcyon days." But in fact your halcyon days might very well lie in the future; the phrase means "period of prosperity" without referring to any particular time—we're just apt to romanticize the past.

Originally "halcyon" didn't even mean "prosperous," but rather "peaceful," which is how people used it until this century. To be precise, "halcyon days" once referred to a fortnight of calm around the winter solstice called *alkyonides hemerai* by the Greeks and *alcyoni dies* by the Romans. The Greeks fancied that a species of birds related to the kingfisher (*alkyon*) nested and bred at sea during the solstice, easing their task by charming the waters calm for two weeks. (The *h* in our spelling of "halcyon" results from a false etymology based on this myth: the Greek *hals-kyoi* means something like "sea-conceiving.")

Behind this tale, as usual, lies another: that of Alcyone, daughter of Aeolus, king of winds. As the story goes, Alcyone made the mistake of marrying Ceyx, son of the Morning Star. So perfect was their marriage that they nicknamed each other "Zeus" and "Hera" (apparently forgetting the divine couple's legendary fights); the gods, taking offense, decided to break up the party. In one version of the tale, they transformed Alcyone into a kingfisher and left her at the seashore. But when the roiling waters threatened to destroy her nest eggs, Zeus took pity, commanding that the seas be still for fourteen days.

Ovid says otherwise. In his version, Ceyx's boat was smashed on a business trip to the Delphic oracle, and he drowned. The next day Alcyone, who had dreamt of the disaster, discovered her husband's body on the shore. Seized with despair, she threw herself into the sea; but both she and her husband were miraculously transformed into halcyons and given the power to calm the waters.

Englishmen, who got the myth mainly from Ovid and Pliny the Elder, initially used "halcyon days" with reference to the fabled fortnight when the oceans are calm. But by the end of the sixteenth century the phrase had also come to refer to any time of peace and quiet. In a book of Christian prayers from 1578, the compiler Richard Day flatters Queen Elizabeth by noting that "it hath pleased thy grace to give us these Alcyon days, which yet we enjoy." Since that time, the old meaning of "halcyon" has slipped into oblivion, though The Upjohn Company must have had it in mind when they gave the name Halcion to their benzodiazepine tranquilizer. It would seem, however, that Halcion's halcyon days have most certainly passed.

A Herculean Effort

The Labors of Hercules · The Nemean Lion
Hydra-Headed · To Cleanse the Augean Stables
The Pillars of Hercules · The Golden Bowl

The Greek champion Heracles—better known to the Romans and to us as Hercules—was something of a Velcro hero. As his cult spread around the Mediterranean, the legends of numerous local strongmen stuck onto him, and his exploits became so numerous that it would take a "Herculean effort" to collect them all. I'm certainly no Heracles, but I'll take on his most famous deeds, the so-called Twelve Labors of Hercules, from which we derive the phrase "Herculean effort."

To begin at the beginning, Heracles was born in Thebes to Queen Alcmene of Tiryns (in Argolis) after Zeus visited her bed in the guise of her husband Amphitryon. Legend has it that it took Zeus and Alcmene three nights to complete the job of conceiving Heracles. In any case he was a mighty offspring, his father's pride and joy, and consequently despised by the jealous Hera. Heracles' prowess was soon put to the test when, in his eighth month, Hera sent a pair of malicious snakes to kill him in his crib. Hardly batting an eye, the infant hero grabbed the snakes and strangled them with his bare hands.

So much for Hera's first assault; there would be plenty more. (And thus the irony of Heracles' name, which means "Hera's glory," and which probably belonged to some historical figure, perhaps a prince of Tiryns, on whom the myths are based.) Sometimes, however, Heracles' travails resulted from his own impetuosity, as when, in a fit of pique, he killed his music tutor with a lute for daring to correct him. For this deed, Amphitryon sent Heracles to tend cattle on a nearby mountain. While there, at age eighteen, Heracles was visited by two beautiful nymphs, Pleasure and Virtue, who offered him a choice between two paths through life—one very pleasant and easy, the other severe but glorious.

Like a fool, Heracles chose the latter, and immediately he found himself confronting a fierce lion. After a mighty struggle, Heracles slew the beast, but a more difficult labor was to follow. He descended the mountain to visit King Thespius of Thespia, only to discover that the king's fondest wish was that each of his fifty daughters would conceive a child by the hero. Heracles reportedly accomplished the task in one night, thus putting Zeus to shame.

Back in Thebes, Heracles married King Creon's daughter Megara, who bore him several admirable children. Everybody was mighty happy with this arrangement, including the gods, who showered many presents on the hero— Hephaestus, for example, gave Heracles the bronze club which would become his emblem, while Apollo bestowed a very handy bow with a quiver of charmed arrows. But then Hera struck again, driving Heracles into a fit of madness which so beguiled him that he murdered his wife and children, imagining they were his enemies. When Heracles came to his senses, he fled Thebes and sought out the oracle at Delphi. The oracle—secretly guided by Hera—instructed him to return to his ancestral home of Tiryns and to purify himself by serving King Eurystheus for twelve years, performing any task he should be assigned. The payoff, the oracle assured him, would be godhood.

Hera, of course, had other plans in mind. She inspired Eurystheus to send Heracles on a series of impossible missions, much as Aphrodite had done to Psyche [see CUPID AND PSYCHE, p. 49]. Both Homer and Hesiod refer to these "Labors of Heracles"—generally involving the killing or capture of some monster—but their number is unspecified; the eventual total of twelve is probably due to tales of the Babylonian sun-god Baal, who reputedly performed a labor while passing through each sign of the zodiac. However their number was arrived at, here are Heracles' labors, in order of performance:

1. THE NEMEAN LION

This beast, a son of Typhon [see A TYPHOON, P. 172], proved relatively easy to dispatch. The lion's skin was invulnerable, so Heracles reverted to a technique he'd discovered in his crib, choking the monster with his arms. He then peeled off the lion's skin with its own claws and wore it as armor. Heracles, thus garbed, must have been a sight when he returned to Tiryns—Eurystheus was so frightened that he crawled into a bronze tub, his habitual retreat whenever Heracles unexpectedly returned from another deadly labor.

2. THE HYDRA OF LERNA

Another of Typhon's offspring, the Hydra was a serpent with anywhere from seven to one hundred heads (the most common figure is nine), specially trained in wickedness by Hera. Heracles was instructed to rid Lerna (near Argos) of this

beast, but, as he discovered, whenever he clubbed off one of its heads, two more grew in its place (thus our expression "hydra-headed," referring to an evil that multiplies with attempts to suppress it). To make matters worse, Hera sent a giant crab as backup support for the Hydra, so Heracles only thought it fair to enlist his nephew Iolaus in the effort. As Heracles cut off each of the Hydra's heads, Iolaus would sear the stump with a brand; meanwhile, Heracles crushed the crab under his foot. The Hydra was finished, but Hera managed to rescue the crab and place it in the sky as the constellation Cancer.

3. THE BOAR OF ERYMANTHUS

Rather a bore, this boar, which Heracles was to bring back alive from Mount Erymanthus (in Arcadia) to Eurystheus. The animal may not have been stronger than Heracles, but it was faster; Zeus's son, however, eventually fatigued the boar by chasing it across various snow-covered fields. Heracles' pursuit was not so hot that he couldn't afford to pay a visit to his friend, the centaur Pholus, a visit that resulted in a good deal of mayhem [*see* THE CENTAURS, p. 145].

4. THE HIND OF CERYNEIA

Heracles' capture of the so-called Hind of Ceryneia—a gold-antlered, bronze-footed deer, sacred to Artemis and native to Arcadia—basically repeats his capture of the boar. In this case, however, the chase took an entire year; and to add insult to injury Artemis got mad at him when he finally caught it. Sometimes a guy just can't win.

5. THE BIRDS OF STYMPHALUS

These nasty creatures, also residents of Arcadia, were sacred to Ares and shared his warlike nature. Their beaks and claws, and even their wings, were brazen, and they could shoot their feathers like arrows at defenseless human beings, whose flesh the birds considered a delicacy. Eurystheus commanded Heracles to drive them from their home base near Stymphalus, for which Athena supplied the hero a bronze rattle. It couldn't have been much of a labor to shake this rattle, but it was sufficient to scare the birds off, and Heracles did shoot some of them down as they attempted to escape.

6. THE AUGEAN STABLES

This was by far the most nauseating labor. A certain Augeas, king of Elis (in the northwestern Peloponnese), possessed a herd of 3,000 cattle, whose stables had not been cleaned for thirty years. Heracles's task was to make up for lost time, and to do it in one day—a feat accomplished when he diverted two rivers through the stables, washing all the filth through the neighbors' backyards. (Ever since, the Augean Stables have served as a metaphor for an extremely disgusting place or situation, and "to cleanse the Augean Stables" now means "to purge filth or corruption.") Bending the rules of Eurystheus's game, Heracles cut a side deal with Augeas for removing the sewage, but Augeas reneged after discovering the true reason Heracles had come. For this slight, Heracles would return to Elis at a later time to wipe out Augeas and his sons, and then allegedly to establish the Olympic Games in honor of his victory.

7. THE CRETAN BULL

The Cretan Bull was originally a gift from the sea-god Poseidon to Minos, the king of Crete most famous for his labyrinth [see THE MINOTAUR, p. 158]. Minos was supposed to sacrifice the bull, but the creature so charmed him that he let it go free, a piece of insubordination Poseidon punished by making the bull run mad, wreaking havoc all over the island. Heracles was posted to Crete to capture the bull, but when he had brought it back to Tiryns he set it loose again to wreak havoc in Greece. The bull would eventually be killed by the Athenian hero Theseus, a legendary figure directly modeled on Heracles.

8. THE HORSES OF DIOMEDES

This Diomedes was not the Trojan War hero, but rather a wicked Thracian king who fed human flesh to his wild mares. Heracles arrived in Diomedes' kingdom of Bistones and, with help from the crew he'd brought along, seized the horses and dragged them to the seacoast. He was pursued, however, by Diomedes' subjects, and while Heracles and his men were distracted by the ensuing fight, the mares ate one of his friends. Enraged, Heracles laid his hands on Diomedes, whom, in a fit of poetic justice, he fed to the wild beasts; this snack so satisfied them that they were instantly tamed.

9. THE GIRDLE OF HIPPOLYTE

One of Eurystheus's daughters heard tell of a beautiful girdle possessed by Hippolyte, queen of the war-like Amazons [*see* p. 97], and soon fell a-coveting. One of Heracles' more de-meaning tasks was fetching this toy for the princess; it was also one of the easiest, since Hippolyte proved surprisingly willing to hand the girdle over. Hera, however, was not about to let Heracles just walk off with the thing, so she stirred up a commotion among the other Amazons, who then attacked him. Thinking himself betrayed by Hippolyte, Heracles killed her after routing the other Amazons. A lot of fuss for a princess's vanity, if you ask me.

10. THE OXEN OF GERYON

Each of Heracles' last three labors involves an escapade at the end of the world and a symbolic conquest of death. The first required the capture of oxen belonging to the three-headed monster Geryon, the offspring of a Gorgon who lived on a fabulous island at the western edge of the earth. For transport, Heracles procured from Helios (the Sun) a charmed vessel known as the Golden Bowl, in which he skimmed across the Mediterranean. Not about to let a mere land mass stand in his way, Heracles plowed through the rocky joint between Africa and Europe, single-handedly opening the Strait of Gibraltar, and raising a mountain to either side, subsequently dubbed "the Pillars of Hercules." Once he attained the island, Heracles made short work of Geryon's two-headed dog Orthrus (another of Typhon's pernicious offspring), Geryon's herdsman, and Geryon himself. He then rode back home with the oxen in the bowl, surmounting numerous obstacles along the way, and surrendering the bowl to Helios at the end.

11. THE APPLES OF THE HESPERIDES

Heracles should have hung on to the Golden Bowl, since Eurystheus's next command was that he head back west and gather up the golden apples of the Hesperides, a task he eventually performed with the help of Atlas. For the story of this labor, see AN ATLAS (p. 14) *and* THE GARDEN OF THE HESPERIDES (p. 190). Along the way, Heracles paid a visit to the bound Titan Prometheus, whom he freed from the dreadful fate of having his liver eaten out by an eagle [*see* p. 43].

12. CERBERUS

Heracles' last labor was easily the most dangerous, since it required him to visit the underworld and drag back the ferocious, three-headed guard-dog Cerberus [*see* p. 170]. On his own, he wouldn't even have been able to cross over the Styx into Hades' kingdom, since that was a journey strictly denied to mortals, but he was accompanied by Hermes and Athena. With their help, Heracles persuaded Hades to let him take Cerberus on a little vacation to Tiryns, provided that he use no weapon to do it. Heracles was again forced to use brute strength, but that proved sufficient, and once he showed Cerberus to the tub-bound Eurystheus, he carried the dog back home. As a side-exploit, he delivered Theseus from the underworld, where Hades had chained him up for attempting to liberate Persephone.

Having thus metaphorically conquered death, Heracles was finally released from his servitude to Eurystheus, but despite the oracle's promise, he had a while to go before immortality. Heracles had no trouble killing time, however, joining in with the Argonauts in the early stages of their expedition [*see* THE GOLDEN FLEECE, p. 192], rescuing a heroine or ten from death, conquering Troy by his lonesome, and joining in the gods' war on the Gigantes. One story in particular deserves mention, since it has to do with his death and apotheosis: the story of his love for Princess Iole of Oechalia, a town in Thessaly.

The first time Heracles set eyes on Iole, he fell madly in love and sought to gain her hand. But Heracles' noble advances and suitorly deeds were spurned by the king and all his sons, save one, Iole's brother Iphitus. Iphitus was thenceforth Heracles' bosom buddy, but when the pair made a trip to Tiryns in search of the king's lost cattle, Hera once again drove Heracles mad, and the besotted hero threw

Iphitus over the city's wall to his death. Hercules was forced to purify himself all over again through servitude, this time to Queen Omphale of Lydia, who required him to wear women's clothes and spin wool for three years while she wore his lion's-skin and brandished his club.

After this humiliating experience, Heracles set off again for home, running into much trouble on the way but also picking up a new wife named Deianira. He did not, however, forget his love for Iole, and it would prove to be his Achilles' heel, ultimately resulting in his death atop Mount Oeta. For the rest of this story, *see* THE CENTAURS, p. 145.

LEDA AND THE SWAN

The myth of Leda and the Swan, to which W. B. Yeats alludes in one of his best-known poems, is more complex than your average tale of Zeus's amours. Behind it lies an older myth, namely that a union between Zeus and Nemesis produced the famous Spartan queen Helen, whose face launched a thousand ships [see A NEMESIS, p. 73, and AN APPLE OF DISCORD, p. 178].

In the revision, which better accords with Trojan War legends, Helen's mother is Queen Leda of Sparta rather than Nemesis. Zeus takes more than a liking to Leda and, when he discovers her bathing, approaches in the guise of a swan. The queen apparently puts up little resistance, though Yeats produced a great poem by imagining otherwise.

Implausibly enough, Leda is already pregnant by her husband, and after joining with Zeus she bears two eggs. One of these hatches Castor and Clytaemnestra (the legitimate children) and the other Pollux and Helen (the bastards). All four would go on to lead illustrious—or infamous—careers. Leda's sons Castor and Pollux ventured with Jason in quest of the Golden Fleece, and were later placed in the heavens as the constellation Gemini. Her daughters, on the other hand, were the ruin of many Greek heroes, Helen by way of launching those ships and Clytaemnestra by way of murdering her husband, the Greek commander Agamemnon.

In case you thought the Greeks had come up with a simple story for a change, you're wrong. The story of Leda and the Swan did not entirely displace the earlier version of Helen's birth, and the contradictions between the two proved bothersome to mythologists. By one compromise account, Nemesis conceives two eggs by Zeus but gives them over to Leda for hatching; by another Leda is transformed into Nemesis after her death. You're free to choose your favorite version, but since Helen caused Troy's destruction it makes good sense that she was a daughter of Nemesis, goddess of divine retribution.

THE MIDAS TOUCH

Half a tale may be better than none, but sometimes the missing half is the important part. Take the legend of the King Midas of Phrygia, son of Gordius (of "Gordian knot" fame). As we all know, Midas was blessed with a "golden touch." What we sometimes forget is that the king was a fool for wanting it, and that he was soon begging to be rid of it. The moral: greed may be deadly.

Midas is the subject of many strange tales, as for example when, in his infancy, the gods inspired a legion of ants to march with grains of wheat into his drooling mouth. This event was taken as a sign that Midas would grow up to be the richest man in the world. Sign or no sign, Midas did indeed amass quite a fortune, which as usual proved a mixed blessing. Midas fell into dissipation and sloth, and his riches only whetted his greed, leading him to make one wish he would soon regret.

It is said that Midas was a great fan of the wine-god Dionysus, and it chanced that one day he was able to do the god a favor. Dionysus's tutor and companion, the perpetually tipsy satyr Silenus, stumbled into Midas's prize rose garden, utterly lost and in no condition to find his way out. Some of Midas's servants rescued Silenus and led him back to court, where he was warmly welcomed and generously feasted. Everyone had a jolly time, but eventually Silenus wished to be returned to Dionysus, so Midas personally led the satyr safely back home.

For this service, Dionysus granted Midas one wish. Midas didn't have to think too long—which turned out to be the problem—before wishing that everything he touched should turn to gold. The results were at first quite pleasant, but the king's so-called Midas touch almost killed him. Gold is good for a lot of things, but it isn't very nutritious; when Midas found that his touch worked even on food he tearfully begged the god to undo the wish. Dionysus had a good laugh and then instructed him to take a bath in the Lydian river Pactolus, which cured Midas but left a huge deposit of gold in the riverbed. (Forget calling your travel agent—all the gold has long since been panned out.)

This should have proved to anyone that Midas lacked a certain judgment, but nonetheless one day the gods Apollo and Pan asked the king to judge a musical contest between them. Apollo strummed out a beautiful tune on his lyre, but Pan more than matched it with his pipe, and Midas judged the latter the victor. Well, you know how vain these gods can be, and Apollo, to let Midas know what he thought of his ears, turned them into those of an ass.

The mortified Midas tried concealing his shame under a large cap, but, as the saying goes, "only his hairdresser knew for sure." The king threatened to do unspeakable things with his barber's shears if the truth ever got out, and you know what torture it is, especially in the beauty shop, to keep a secret to yourself. Unable to endure this torment for long, the barber made his way to a remote spot, dug a hole in the ground, whispered into it that "Midas has the ears of an ass," then quickly filled the hole back up. This relieved his burden, but on that spot grew a reed that evermore whispered to each passerby the king's shameful secret.

There are other, less fantastic, tales about Midas, most of them borrowed from an actual Phrygian king of the same name who ruled in the late eighth century B.C. This Midas, for example, is said to have committed suicide by drinking the blood of an ox as his kingdom was overrun by the Cimmerians, a northern Asiatic people. Perhaps the real-life Midas inspired his namesake's legends, as Greek storytellers applied their golden touch to the rather less amusing materials of history.

MYRRH

If myrrh hadn't been among the gifts of the biblical three Magi, Westerners would hardly know of it, since it is native only to the Orient (principally India, but also Arabia and eastern Africa). Myrrh is an aromatic resin, now used in perfumes and incense, but it is also the common name of the genus of trees and shrubs—in particular, *Commiphora myrrha*—which produce the gum.

The Greek word *myrrha* has Semitic roots, and along with the name the Greeks imported a myth. The myrrh tree began life, in Syrian legend, as Myrrha, the daughter of King Cinyras of Paphos (in Cyprus). The princess somehow ran afoul of the goddess Aphrodite, who took revenge by firmly lodging in Myrrha's breast a lust for her own father.

Torn between passion and shame, Myrrha was on the verge of suicide when her nurse Hippolyta intervened. In Ovid's version, Hippolyta found the perfect opportunity to help in the annual festival of the goddess Ceres, when all mothers were required to absent their husbands' beds for nine nights. Hippolyta offered to procure Cinyras a substitute, a fetching young virgin of about the same age as his own daughter. Cinyras was happy to oblige, and under the cover of darkness the foul deed was consummated.

Cinyras was so satisfied with his little concubine that he called her back several more times, until curiosity got the better of him. One night he brought a lamp so he could see exactly whom he was making time with, only to be horror-struck by his discovery [*compare and contrast* CUPID AND PSYCHE, p. 49]. Paying his own sins no mind, Cinyras drew his sword on Myrrha, who took to her heels and didn't stop running until she reached Arabia.

With Cinyras in the dust, Myrrha collapsed. Wishing to be neither left alive to shame the living nor killed and thus sent down under to outrage the dead, Myrrha begged the gods to arrange for something in between. Slowly she felt her feet become roots, her limbs branches, her blood sap, and her skin bark; her tears of shame turned to gum, oozing profusely from the trunk. Myrrha had become a myrrh tree.

But there's more to the story. Inside her trunk a child was growing; and for the story of what happened to him once he broke out, *see* p. 95.

ORPHIC

When spelled with a small o, "orphic" broadly means "mystical" or "occult." But once upon a time, "Orphism" was the name of a specific doctrine, groundbreaking in its day, allegedly handed down by the legendary bard Orpheus.

The Greeks considered Orpheus their greatest poet before Homer; he was supposed to have lived in Thrace during the so-called Heroic Age—the days when Heracles, Theseus, Jason, and the rest roamed the world performing great deeds. It was said that Orpheus was a son of the golden-throated Muse Calliope, and that as a youth he was befriended by the god Apollo. Apollo presented the boy with a charmed lyre, which the Muses taught him to play so well that his song could move stones, trees, and even mountains, and, à la the Pied Piper, soothe the fiercest beasts. Orpheus's musical powers came in handy when he joined the Argonauts in their quest for the Golden Fleece [see p. 192]—in one case he saved the crew from the Sirens by belting out a tune even more enchanting than theirs.

After returning home from this expedition, Orpheus married the charming tree-nymph Eurydice, whose beauty also earned her the unwelcome attention of a minor god named Aristaeus. While fleeing Aristaeus, Eurydice chanced to step on a snake, whose retaliatory bite killed her. Orpheus was so bereaved that he resolved to either carry Eurydice back from the underworld or die in the attempt. So he made his way to the kingdom of Hades and Persephone, where he so enchanted the royal couple with his song that they readily agreed to let Eurydice go free. But there was one condition: as Orpheus led his wife home, he was not to look back at her until they reached the world of the living.

Of course, like Lot's wife before him, Orpheus blew it. Even as they were on the verge of crossing back into this world, he let his anxiety get the better of him, and when he turned to look back at Eurydice she vanished without a trace. When his petition to try again was rebuffed, Orpheus returned home in a black mood. There he grew to loathe the company of men and especially of women, and then made the mistake of ill-treating the Thracian devotees of Dionysus, who were known as "Bacchantes" or "maenads" ("mad-women"; see DIONYSIAN, p. 22). The Maenads whipped themselves up into a Dionysian fury and took revenge on the uncivil bard by tearing him to pieces and throwing his head into the river Hebrus. Orpheus's head rode the current into the sea, crying out "Eurydice! Eurydice!" as it went, until it landed on the island of Lesbos, whose inhabitants would subsequently become the first great masters of the lyre. (The gods rescued Orpheus's original, placing it in the sky as the constellation Lyra.)

Orpheus was gone but not forgotten, especially since various poems attributed to him were later compiled and passed off as the source of a great mystical doctrine known as "Orphism." Flourishing in Greece during the sixth century B.C., Orphism departed from traditional religion by stressing individual guilt and redemption—thus disposing with the alibis of fate and divine intervention. The so-called "followers of Orpheus" were big on ritual purification, believed in a form of reincarnation, and, ironically enough, were espe-

cially devoted to the god Dionysus. One of their rituals even involved tearing animals to pieces, much as the maenads had destroyed their supposed master.

As it turns out, however, even if Orpheus existed, his teachings were for the most part invented by later Greek poets; furthermore, several of the surviving Orphic texts were actually forged by early Christian grammarians. Nonetheless, the name "Orphic" stuck to the doctrine, and when over time Orpheus came to be regarded as a man of divine foresight as well as mystical wisdom, "Orphic" came to mean "oracular" and "occult" in general.

A PROCRUSTEAN BED

If you are at all acquainted with academic or political rhetoric, you will no doubt be familiar with the metaphor "a Procrustean bed," an insult regularly hurled against catchall theories and various "-isms." Simply put, a Procrustean bed is any model or idea into which someone tries to stretch or squeeze very different things. If the data don't agree with the model, they have to be "reinterpreted"; complexities and contradictions likewise require "simplification."

No modern-day Procrustean bed, however, is as uncomfortable as the original, which belonged to the ruthless brigand Procrustes, whose name roughly means "the Stretcher" in Greek. (He had several aliases, such as Damastes, "the Overcomer.") Procrustes dwelt in Eleusis, somewhat west of Athens, and if you fell into his clutches you were in for a lot of trouble.

First Procrustes would rob you blind and carry you home and then, out of sheer deviltry, tie you down to a special bed designed for discomfort. If you happened to be as tall as the bed was long, you might expect only routine torture; but if you were shorter, Procrustes would hammer and stretch you out until you fit exactly, and if you were taller he would lop off the excess. This was, to say the least, a disturbed fellow.

Procrustes would have indulged himself until doomsday had it not been for the hero Theseus, who happened to pass through Eleusis on his way to Athens, where he expected to claim his birthright as prince. Theseus fancied himself another Heracles, and he used this journey to make a name for himself by eliminating various monsters and criminals. He had already dispatched, among others, the villainous Sinis, who amused himself by tying captives to two bent pine trees which, when released, tore the victims in half. (Perhaps you notice a theme here.) Suffice it to say, Theseus gave better than he got from Procrustes, whom he tortured to death in the same way Procrustes had tortured his own victims.

Once safely dead, Procrustes passed into metaphor, and his name began showing up in English by the late sixteenth century. The phrase "Procrustean bed," however, dates only to the nineteenth century, when it was employed by the novelist Elizabeth Gaskell and later by Benjamin Jowett, the great translator of Plato. Jowett was the first to put the phrase to what is now its most common use when he insisted that we must not "confine the Platonic dialogue on the Procrustean bed of a single idea." So much for the Intro to Philosophy course you took in college.

PYGMALION

If you think you know which is the oldest profession, think again. According to Ovid, prostitution was preceded by sculpture, among other things; at least, that's the gist of his version of the legend of Pygmalion, a king of Cyprus who, according to the Greeks, married a statue of the goddess Aphrodite.

In Ovid's racier version, Pygmalion is a decent king but an even better sculptor. It happened that during his reign Aphrodite got fed up with the human sacrifices then fashionable on the island, one of her earthly pieds-à-terre; so she punished the Cypriots by opening the first whorehouses in history. The original prostitutes behaved in so disgusting a fashion that King Pygmalion forever renounced the company of females, channeling his energy into sculpture instead.

But the more he tried to forget about women the more obsessed he became; Pygmalion willy-nilly spent most of his time sculpting well-endowed female figures. One of these statues was so astoundingly beautiful that he actually fell in love with it, whispering little nothings in its ear, planting kisses on its stony lips, and caressing its smooth form, all the while fantasizing that it was not only alive but also compliant. But at the crucial moment Pygmalion would always run smack into reality, which as you can imagine got to be pretty frustrating.

As the yearly festival of Aphrodite approached, Pygmalion, only just daring to hope, sacrificed a bull and prayed that the goddess would send him a wife who was the living likeness of his beloved statue. Aphrodite divined Pygmalion's true wish, and as he lay down beside his creation she brought it slowly to life: its body grew warm, its skin turned soft beneath his touch, and finally its lips returned his kiss. Pygmalion rejoiced, and hurried his now-living creation to the nearest altar to make their marriage official.

This charming tale of narcissistic wish fulfillment gained special notoriety at the end of the sixteenth century, when the English satirist John Marston produced a poetic adaptation even more prurient than the original. (Marston's poem was perhaps the chief cause of a huge book-burning party thrown in 1599 by England's leading bishops.) Response was somewhat tamer to two more recent versions of the tale, George Bernard Shaw's sociological play *Pygmalion* and its Broadway adaptation *My Fair Lady*.

A Sisyphean Task

In Book 11 of Homer's *Odyssey*, Odysseus describes, among the torments suffered in the underworld by various legendary men, that of Sisyphus, whose eternal task is to push a huge stone up a hellish hill. Of course, the stone always rolls right back down to the bottom each time he's reached the top. This is his "Sisyphean task," a phrase we now apply to hopeless and constantly frustrating ventures.

Homer apparently counted on his audience to know how Sisyphus earned this punishment, since he doesn't explain it. We gather from the *Iliad* that Sisyphus is the son of a certain Aeolus (a descendent of Deucalion) and the grandfather of Bellerophon [see PEGASUS, p. 162], but we have to rely on later writings for the rest of the story. What we find, predictably enough, are themes with many variations.

A composite account goes something like this: just off the Greek isthmus, Sisyphus founded a new settlement (later called Corinth) as a base for various thievish operations. He was both clever (his name means "the Crafty One") and heartless, not only ransacking neighboring towns but also burying his victims under heaps of stones. The gods let such cruelties pass, but eventually Sisyphus slipped up.

One day Zeus passed through Corinth with his latest paramour and advised Sisyphus to keep their whereabouts strictly hush-hush. But when the girl's father, the river-god Asopus, showed up on Sisyphus's doorstep, the crafty one uncraftily spilled the beans in return for a nice little spring near his palace. Zeus, enraged, sent Thanatos (Death) after

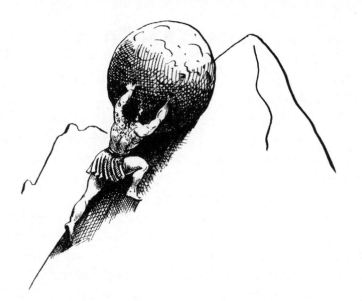

the stool pigeon, but Sisyphus managed to slip some magical chains around Thanatos while he wasn't looking.

Sisyphus had a good laugh over this caper, which had the additional result of removing the Greeks' fear of death and thus of the gods. Zeus soon dispatched Ares to free Thanatos, who then lit out after his captor. But Sisyphus had one more trick up his sleeve: he instructed his wife to neglect the traditional funeral rites once Thanatos had taken him off.

Upon arriving in the underworld, Sisyphus complained bitterly of his wife's neglect, persuading Persephone to let him return and straighten things out. Once free, Sisyphus refused to return, having yet another laugh at the gods before Hermes carted him back to the underworld for keeps. Zeus was determined not to be made a fool of again and thus devised the "Sisyphean task," which he rightly figured would keep the trickster too busy to plot another escape.

Appealing to the curious logic of mythical thought, later writers claimed that this clever antihero must be the father of the most clever Greek of the Heroic Age, namely Odysseus. Contradicting Homer's poems outright, they explained that Sisyphus fathered Odysseus by the daughter of Hermes' son Autolycus, the most famous thief in all Greek myth. One would think that ascribing so evil a father to so famous a hero would cause the Greeks some embarrassment, but it is easy to see why it would appeal to later Christian writers, who tended to regard Odysseus as too clever by half.

As for Sisyphus, he escaped the underworld again, toward the end of the sixteenth century, to bask in the light of English literature. The proverb "to roll Sisyphean stones" soon emerged, but it would take until the 1870s before such phrases as "Sisyphean toil" and "Sisyphean labor" were coined. These are the ancestors of the now more common expression "Sisyphean task," which thanks to Albert Camus became a catchphrase to an entire angst-ridden generation.

In the December 1991 issue of *Spy* magazine, Charlotte Allen and Charlotte Hays nicely balance two mythological phrases in one sentence. In a piece on the U.S. administration's exertions on behalf of Vice President Dan Quayle, the object of many unkind cuts, the authors note that overcoming his negative image was both initially daunting and ultimately hopeless. "Thus," they write, "what started as a Herculean effort to mold a better image for the vice president has turned Sisyphean. His staff has labored mightily . . . [but] at every juncture, Quayle says or does something that makes them cringe or crumple."

To Sow Dragon's Teeth

This strange metaphor for stirring up a ruckus traces to the legend of Cadmus, reputed founder of Thebes (now called Thivai), a city in east-central Greece. Cadmus was a son of King Agenor of Tyre in Phoenicia and thus the brother of Europa [see p. 103]. When Zeus took a liking to the princess and furtively whisked her off to Crete, Agenor dispatched his sons and advised them not to return without her.

Now, it was no trouble for Zeus to keep a lover hidden (except from his own wife), so naturally Cadmus found no trace of Europa anywhere. He finally made his way to Delphi to ask Apollo for help; instead of revealing Europa's whereabouts, the oracle, knowing Cadmus could never go home, instructed him to follow a certain heifer until she flopped down on the ground, and to settle on that spot. Cadmus obeyed, following the beast to the region of Greece called Boeotia (from *bous*, "cow") and building there what would become the Theban citadel.

The first thing to do was to offer a sacrifice. Cadmus had the cow, but he lacked water (needed for purification), so he sent his men out in search of a spring. They found one close by, but as it happened this spring was sacred to the god Ares, who had set one of his sons, a dragon, to guard it. The monster made quick work of Cadmus's men, but when Cadmus himself came looking he managed to crush the beast's head with a rock. On the instant, the goddess Athena appeared to applaud him, chipping in the curious suggestion that Cadmus sow the dragon's teeth in the soil near the spring.

Once Cadmus had sown the teeth, a race of fearsome men sprouted up, all armed to the hilt. The frightened hero, from his hiding place, cleverly tossed a stone in their midst, setting off a huge argument over who had thrown what at whom. The result was a bloody slaughter; when the dust settled, only Cadmus and five of these men were left standing. Rather than finish each other off they decided to return to the citadel and found a city. These men, called "Spartoi" (the Sown), were supposed in later times to be the ancestors of Thebes' leading families. (Cadmus's triumph inspired the phrase "Cadmean victory," which, given the carnage, is synonymous with "Pyrrhic victory.")

Meanwhile, however, Ares was in a rage over his son's demise, and he demanded compensation. Cadmus agreed to serve the god for eight years, but this did not entirely assuage him. A lingering curse led to several bizarre events too

complex to get into here, but suffice it to say that Cadmus and his wife Harmonia passed their old age as snakes on the Fortunate Isles [see p. 185]. In the interim, Cadmus had introduced the sixteen-letter Phoenician alphabet to Greece (where it was called the "Cadmean alphabet") and had fathered Semele, mother by Zeus of the wine-god Dionysus.

Though most classicists would tell you that the Greeks adapted the Phoenician syllabary between the tenth and eighth centuries B.C., Herodotus claims that Cadmus's adventures took place about 1,000 years earlier, which means that it would take nearly four millennia for an Englishman to recognize their literary potential. John Milton was the first, in his *Areopagitica* (1644), to mention the dragon's teeth; but it was John Marsden who, in his *History of the Early Puritans* (1853), coined the catchphrase. "Jesuits," he notes polemically, "sowed the dragon's teeth which sprung up into the hydras of rebellion and apostasy." In the heat of his argument, Marsden mixes both myths and metaphors.

To Tantalize

Perhaps you should think twice the next time someone makes you a "tantalizing" offer. Because Tantalus, the first man ever tantalized, would probably rather have tangoed with Medusa or played fetch with Cerberus.

In the beginning, Tantalus, a Lydian king and son of Zeus, was merely another mortal. But his parentage made him vain and reckless, and somewhere along the line (accounts differ) Tantalus overstepped himself. According to one tale, he blabbed some divine secrets his father had confided over dinner; in another, he filched some nectar and ambrosia right off the gods' table and helped himself to immortality. Worse, like some Greek Robin Hood, he spread the divine food among his Lydian cronies.

But the best and bloodiest story is that Tantalus decided one day to match wits with the gods and invited them over for a feast. Tantalus slaved over a hot cauldron, carefully mincing his son Pelops to pieces and boiling them up, adding salt to taste. Once the gods had arrived and polished off a few cocktails, Tantalus sat them down to dinner.

After passing a few awkward glances, the gods refused even to play with their food, having been not in the least bit taken by the ruse. Demeter, however, was too busy fretting over the loss of her daughter Persephone [see GO TO HADES, p. 33] to pay any attention to what she was eating—which happened to be Pelops's shoulder. Annoyed at his son's stupid joke, Zeus commanded that the boiled pieces be thrown back into the cauldron and, in a process that must have looked like a film run backward, conjured up a restored Pelops. The boy did lack a shoulder, but Demeter offered an ivory prosthetic as compensation. It is said that each of Pelops's descendents, as a peculiar birthmark, bore one shoulder as white as ivory.

Then Zeus turned on the cook. Since Tantalus was now immortal, the god devised for him a fate worse than death, namely to be eternally ravaged by unquenchable thirst and insatiable hunger. To heighten the torture, Zeus placed Tantalus up to his neck in a river, whose waters receded whenever he bent his head to drink. And though boughs laden with succulent fruit hung just within reach, whenever Tantalus attempted to pick some a wind blew the fruit away.

Thus the depressing origins of our word "tantalize," which when first used in the sixteenth century still implied "to torture." You might think Tantalus's kin had learned their lesson, but you'd be wrong. Pelops himself, alive and in one piece only by the gods' good graces, would go on to murder one of Hermes' sons, thus bringing down a curse on his house. Various gruesome murders resulted, one of them even involving another human-flesh recipe. Pelops's great-grandson Orestes finally put an end to the family fun by propitiating the Furies [see p. 35], and that puts an end to this entry.

BEASTS,
MONSTERS,
AND DEMONS

ARGUS-EYED

Zeus, up to his usual tricks, has fallen for one of his wife's devotees: Princess Io of Argos, a Peloponnesian seaside kingdom. Hera, smelling trouble, whisks herself to Argos for a look-see; Zeus, desperate to cover his tracks, turns Io into a cow. It was a nice try. The suspicious goddess admires the beast and then demands her as a gift; though it breaks his heart, Zeus can't refuse without blowing his cover. Thus Hera leads Io off and sets her under the ever-watchful eyes of the monstrous Argus—and I do mean *eyes*.

Some say Argus (a.k.a. Argos) was the great-grandson of another Argos, ancestor of the family that ruled his name-sake kingdom—Argus the younger would thus, ironically, be Io's relative. He was said not only to have been massive and mighty, but also, if you believe certain poets, to have had eyes all over his body, literally hundreds of them.

So the plaintively mooing Io could never evade Argus's gaze, especially since only two eyes slept at a time, leaving the rest on duty. Argus was, in short, "Argus-eyed," that is, "ever watchful." Though the myth had already been known to Europeans for several hundred years, the epithet first appears in English in John Florio's 1603 translation of Montaigne, who observes that "No human judgment is so . . . Argus-eyed, but sometimes shall fall asleep."

Apparently, Zeus hoped Argus wasn't so Argus-eyed, either. Not to be outdone by Hera, he charged his son Hermes to put her watchman out of the picture. Disguised as a shepherd, Hermes sidled up to Argus and piped on an enchanted reed, aiming to lull the rest of his eyes to sleep. But steely-willed Argus successfully resisted. Hermes then fell back on a more effective method, launching into a lengthy chronicle of his pipe's history. This time Argus succumbed, and as soon as every eye was sealed, Hermes lopped off his head.

This deed didn't sit especially well with Hera, who took revenge by pestering the freed but still bovine Io with Argus's ghost—or a Fury, or a mighty big gadfly, depending on which version you prefer. Eventually Zeus broke down, swearing to Hera he'd never betray her again. Whether or not she believed this (it was false), she gave in, allowing her husband to restore Io (then in Egypt) to human form, and then later to make her a bona-fide goddess.

Argus, however, was quite thoroughly dead; the grieving Hera could only save his eyes, which she set in the tail of her favorite bird, the peacock. "Argus" has since become the name of a species of pheasant.

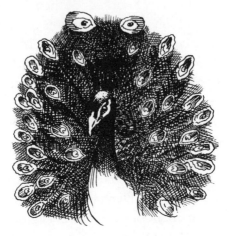

THE CENTAURS

Rowdy, lustful, rude, and quickly intoxicated, the Centaurs were the Greeks' Greeks—the frat boys of the classical world. Hailing from the mountains of Thessaly (northeastern Greece), these barbaric creatures—among the earliest cross-breeds in classical myth—had horses' bodies where their legs should have been, and the brains to match.

But this may be unfair to the Centaurs, who were perhaps more "civilized" than the Greeks who called them barbarians. It's possible that what looked from a distance like a horse with the upper body of a man was just a foreign cowboy ("Centaur" means "bull-goader")—a mystifying sight if you haven't yet learned to tame horses.

Maybe. But maybe what the myths say is true: that the Centaurs were engendered in the blind passion the Thessalian hero Ixion expended on a Hera-shaped cloud—a blasphemy earning him a place of dishonor in Tartarus, strapped to a flaming wheel. Either way, the Centaurs were objects of constant derision in Greek literature. Homer, for example, calls them "hairy beast men" and accuses them of having disrupted a royal Thessalian wedding ceremony by getting stone drunk and attempting to rape all the women. As a result they were trounced and driven out of Thessaly.

The quintessential bad guests, the Centaurs were equally bad hosts. When Heracles visited the relatively hospitable Centaur Pholus, the latter, at Heracles' request, uncapped a communal wine jar. Since Centaurs could smell the grape from a mile away, the rest came running. They forgot the gods had given them the jar only on the condition that they always treat Heracles well, and proceeded to attack him for daring to take a nip. They were trounced once again.

The Centaurs were bad losers too, and eventually they paid Heracles back—not that it did them much good. One day, after accidentally offing an in-law and thus being forced into exile, Heracles and his new wife Deianira chanced upon the river Evenus, where the Centaur Nessus ran a small business carrying travelers across.

Deciding to ford the river himself, Heracles foolishly entrusted his wife to Nessus, who, being a Centaur, of course attempted to rape her. This outrage prompted Heracles to shoot Nessus dead with an arrow poisoned in the Hydra's blood [see p. 111]. Before expiring, however, Nessus offered Deianira his coat, which he claimed had the power to keep Heracles forever faithful. What he didn't say is that the coat, being soaked in his blood, was poisoned too.

Now it happened that Heracles had a long-standing crush on a certain Princess Iole, whom he finally managed to spirit off to a mountaintop, where he intended to celebrate his catch by building an altar to Zeus. Realizing he wasn't properly dressed for the occasion, Heracles sent word home requesting a ceremonial tunic.

The jealous Deianira, recalling the Centaur's promise, thought she could kill two birds with one tunic. So she sent Nessus's coat, which Heracles blithely slipped on only to discover that it burned his flesh and was impossible to remove. As the poison seeped through his skin, the agonized hero fell cursing to the ground, begging Zeus to deliver him from this torture. When nothing happened, Heracles ordered his attendants to end his misery by setting him afire.

Zeus looked on, admiring his son's courage and reminiscing over Heracles' many mighty deeds. These thoughts eventually prompted the god to intervene. Snatching Heracles from the flames, Zeus whisked him up to Olympus where, to the applause of all assembled, he made his son a god. So while Nessus had his revenge, it ultimately backfired; those poor Centaurs couldn't do anything right.

A CHIMERA

The people of Lycia (an Asian kingdom), having apparently outraged some god or other, wake up one day to find themselves pestered by a fearsome creature called the "Chimera," from the Greek for "little she-goat." Far from being cuddly as her name would imply, the Chimera was a fire-breathing and irritable beast with the head of a lion, the midsection of a goat, and the hindquarters of a dragon. Some say she sported the heads of all three, and others that the goat's head grew out of her back. Any way you cut it, this pest was mighty ugly. (In addition to being nasty in herself, the Chimera also mothered two other terrors: the Sphinx and the Nemean Lion—*see* pp. 168, 111.)

To make matters worse, the Lycian king, Iobates, has another problem on his hands, namely the hero Bellerophon. There's bad blood between Bellerophon and Iobates' brother-in-law, King Proteus of Argos, and though the hero doesn't

know it Proteus has ordered Iobates to kill him. Bellerophon's reluctant host figures he can dispose of both problems by sending his guest to slay the Chimera, expecting the two to make mutual mincemeat.

But the gods are with Bellerophon, at least for the moment, so Athena supplies him with a charmed bridle and a winged horse named Pegasus [see p. 162]. With Pegasus's help, Bellerophon polishes off the Chimera and returns triumphant to the chagrined Iobates. It won't be long, however, before the hero's vanity brings down Nemesis and the wrath of a few other gods; two of his children are killed, and he's deposited on an Asian plain to eat his heart out.

English references to the Chimera pop up by the fourteenth century, as for example in John Wyclif's prologue to his edition of the Bible. (He dismisses the beast as a heathen fantasy.) By the sixteenth century, the Chimera had become a metaphor for any wild and fearsome illusion, especially if patched together from incongruous sources (just as the original was compounded from three beasts). This metaphor gave rise to the phrase "to chase a chimera," meaning "to pursue a foolish fantasy."

The beast herself, however, was not entirely a fantasy. She seems to have personified a Lycian volcano—a fire-breathing mountain—which in its upper reaches was home to lions, in its middle region to goats, and at its base to snakes. The volcano was also called "Chimera," but whether it explains the myth or the myth explains its name and description is now impossible to say.

A CYCLOPS

You probably think that the Cyclopes (plural of "Cyclops") were big, dumb, hairy brutes with one eye and a taste for raw flesh. But that's just so much Homeric propaganda. In fact, according to Hesiod, the Cyclopes were big, hairy brutes with one eye who were handy with a forge.

One can be sure, at least, that these monsters lacked a second eyeball, since the name "Cyclops" means "round eye" in the emphatic singular. But the two earliest Greek poets part ways on a lot of the other details. Hesiod claims the Cyclopes were three in number and sons of Gaia and Uranus, which made them brothers of the Titans. Their father was no big fan of theirs, and, smelling trouble, saw to it that the Cyclopes were safely chained up at an early age. The Titan Cronus deduced that his muscular, round-eyed siblings might be of some aid in his bid to take power [see TITANIC, p. 6], so he freed the Cyclopes, only to cast them down into Tartarus once he was safely in power.

Was ever a trio so grievously abused? Happily, Zeus proved more grateful after liberating them to help overthrow the Titans. In that rebellion and afterward the Cyclopes applied their skill to hammer out Zeus's thunderbolts, his deadliest weapons. For good measure they fashioned Hades' cap of invisibility and Poseidon's awesome trident. Alas, for such loyal service they would meet their end at Apollo's hands, after Zeus used a thunderbolt to strike down the sun-god's son Asclepius [see APOLLONIAN, p. 20].

Homer's Cyclopes, though also gigantic and also one-eyed, are an altogether different, and far more numerous, crew.

Where they came from and exactly where they lived the poet does not say, though later writers made Sicily their home. These Cyclopes, not particularly civilized or inventive, were shepherds, feeding off the raw meat of their flocks despite being at least smart enough to build a fire. (Agriculture was way beyond them.) When the opportunity presented itself, they would also indulge their taste for raw human flesh, and one day a big opportunity arrived in the form of the hero Odysseus and his crew.

This windfall befell the Cyclops named Polyphemus, a son of Poseidon and something of a loner. When Polyphemus spies the Greeks, who had recklessly ventured into his cave, he demands to know their business; Odysseus, after bragging a bit about his military exploits, begs for much-needed provisions. Polyphemus responds by grabbing two Greeks, dashing them on the ground, and eating them. He imprisons the rest in his cave, making a meal out of another four before Odysseus manages to drive a huge, smouldering poker in the drunkenly dozing Cyclops's eye.

Polyphemus runs bawling to his compatriots, blaming his distress on "No Man," the phony name Odysseus had shrewdly given him. "If no man hurts you," they reply, "then your plight must be the will of Zeus. So be it." Polyphemus gropes his way back to the cave and rolls away the stone blocking its entrance, hoping to slaughter his persecutors; but the Greeks cleverly escape by clinging to the bellies of sheep as they file out of the cave. The joke would have been on Polyphemus if Odysseus, back on ship with his men, hadn't felt it necessary to taunt the monster, boasting of his wit and revealing his true name. Being Poseidon's son, the Cyclops has some recourse: he begs his father to make Odysseus's trip home a living hell, and the sea-god responds with a vengeance.

This isn't the Greeks' last word on the Cyclopes. Blending some of the details from Homer's and Hesiod's stories, they depicted the round-eyes as servants of the fire-god Hephaestus in his workshop beneath Mt. Aetna on Sicily [see A VOLCANO]. Some writers claimed these Cyclopes had built, out of stones whose proportions defied human strength, the great prehistoric walls and fortifications that the Greeks found in ruins. This detail may owe something to Hesiod's claim that the Cyclopes had three brothers by Uranus and Gaia named the Hecatoncheires ("Hundred-handers"), each of them also having fifty heads and "mighty, invincible strength." If there's anybody I'd less rather meet in a dark alley than a Cyclops, it's one of these guys.

A HARPY

Has the wind ever snatched a twenty-dollar bill from your hand, or blown a sweetheart's letter into the gutter? The Greeks had a name for such thieving winds: *Harpyiai*, "the Snatchers." According to Homer, not only could these Harpies steal your hat, they could steal you too, whisk you off to the underworld and deliver you up to their masters, the vengeful Furies [*see* p. 35].

Whenever the Greeks got the idea that some disembodied natural force was actually a god or spirit, they eventually gave it a body and features, if only so they could draw pictures. Hesiod got the ball rolling by observing off-hand that the Snatchers had wings and very nicely styled hair; not much, but a start. Artists, taking off from Hesiod, depicted the Harpies as vulture-like creatures with the heads of maidens, faces twisted and pale with hunger, and claws that were long, sharp, and grasping. They also smelled really bad.

Friendly is not what you'd call these monsters, though they did prove useful to the Furies and sundry other gods. Take the case of the Thracian soothsayer Phineus, who—already blind for having crossed Zeus—angered the gods a second time by putting out his sons' eyes. For this rash act, Phineus was plagued with the Harpies, who snatched away and then fouled whatever food was put on his table. Eventually Zeus permitted two Argonauts to rescue him, and the Harpies were driven off to stir up trouble elsewhere.

It was Virgil's description of the Harpies that, in the early sixteenth century, first caught the English imagination. And once these monsters got to be known, like other mythological figures they soon got turned into metaphors. Rapacious persons, especially rapacious women, were cavalierly dubbed "harpies"; somewhat later (in 1859) William Makepeace Thackeray used the word in the way now characteristic: "Was it my mother-in-law, the grasping, odious, abandoned, barren harpy?" (*The Virginians*, chapter 18). Slightly earlier, a South American bird of prey had been dubbed the "harpy-eagle," "harpy" for short, and slightly later an East Indian bat would be called the "harpy-bat." But in common speech the word is now reserved for mothers-in-law and other female tormentors.

MEDUSA'S HEAD

The Gorgons (from the Greek for "terrible"), three offspring of the sea-god Phorcys and his sister Ceto, were indeed a sight *not* to behold. How ugly were they? With their bronze claws, massive teeth, and heads adorned with snakes instead of hair, they were so ugly that one look would turn you to stone. Though all three were equally dangerous, only Medusa, the mortal Gorgon, became famous, mostly by way of the story of her death, which goes something like this:

King Acrisius of Argos, informed by an oracle that his daughter Danaë will bear a son who would someday kill him, shuts her up in a bronze tower and throws away the key. Good enough to keep out mere men; but when Zeus takes a liking to somebody a lock is hardly going to stop him. The god rains himself into Danaë's cell in a shower of gold, and nine months later she gives birth to a son named Perseus.

Foiled, Acrisius then shuts up his daughter and Perseus in a trunk and tosses it to the sea. The gods, however, are not about to let their sacred decree be so easily circumvented, so they guide the trunk to the island kingdom of Seriphus, where its contents are taken to King Polydectes. But Perseus isn't out of the soup just yet, since Polydectes falls in love with Danaë and wants her bothersome offspring out of the picture. He commands Perseus to get him Medusa's head and thus rid the kingdom of a notorious pest. (Compare the adventures of Bellerophon—*see* A CHIMERA, p. 148.)

The hero, though dumb enough to take the job, is smart enough to go prepared. With Athena and Mercury backing him up, Perseus first visits the Graeae, three prematurely gray sisters of the Gorgons, and extorts from them a few magical items to facilitate his work, including winged sandals, à la Mercury's, an enchanted sack, and the famous "Cap of Hades," which rendered its wearer invisible. Hermes pitches in with a sickle, and Athena with a reflective shield.

With this load it's amazing that Perseus could still walk; but he does manage to track down Medusa, whom he discovers asleep. Donning the Cap of Hades, Perseus approaches his target backward while observing her in Athena's shield—only Medusa's direct gaze was deadly. One quick chop with the sickle, and Perseus bags her head in the magic sack. The other Gorgons awaken in confusion, and then wax furious, but since they can't see Perseus there's little they are going to do about it.

After a few more amazing exploits and diverting encounters, Perseus returns to Seriphus, where his mother is in flight from the now openly nasty Polydectes. Perseus corners the king and pulls Medusa's head out of the sack, turning him into a hunk of rock. Back on the road, Perseus ends up in the Thessalian kingdom of Larissa, where he takes part in the athletic games being held in honor of a special guest. Perseus goes a little overboard with a discus, which smashes into the special guest's foot and kills him. Who was this guest? Perhaps you've guessed it was Acrisius himself.

Thus the Fates finally foiled the foolish king, managing to pack Medusa off to Tartarus in the bargain. As for Medusa's head, Perseus reportedly donated it to Athena, who placed it in her shield [see UNDER THE AEGIS, p. 203]. Today, Medusa's Head can be found as a cluster of stars in the constellation Perseus.

THE MINOTAUR

A LABYRINTH · TO MEANDER · ARIADNE'S THREAD
THE AEGEAN SEA

It is well known that the culturally insecure Romans borrowed heavily from the Greeks. It is less well known that the Greeks themselves looked to the East for help—especially to Minoan Crete, whose culture flourished in the earlier half of the second millennium B.C.

This period is called "Minoan" after a certain Cretan king or dynasty of kings called Minos, later collapsed by the Greeks into a single legendary figure, sometimes into two (one Minos being the other's grandfather). You will be asked to assume a lot as this tale unfolds, so let's assume for now that Minos was a single man. He was said to have been a son, along with Rhadamanthus, of Zeus and Europa [see p. 103], and the two boys were adopted when a Cretan king married their mother. When this king died Minos bid for the throne, claiming the gods favored him; as proof, he prayed to Poseidon to bring forth an animal from the waters. The sea-god delivered a bull, on the condition that Minos promptly sacrifice it to him; but the animal was so lovely that the new king couldn't bring himself to do it.

This was his first mistake. Poseidon, insulted, drove Minos's wife Pasiphaë into a raging passion for the handsome bull. Pasiphaë, at her wits' end, appealed for help to the clever craftsman Daedalus, who fashioned a wooden shell in the shape of a buxom cow. Pasiphaë crawled into the contraption and let out her best approximation of a mating call, which brought the bull running and consummated Poseidon's revenge.

In the appropriate time Pasiphaë brought forth a monstrous son, having the body of a man and the head of a bull, known as "Minotaurus" or simply as "the Minotaur" ("Minos's bull"). As yet unaware of Daedalus's role in the affair, Minos instructed him to build a huge maze, in the center of which the king could hide the Minotaur and thus his shame. Taking a cue from the famously intricate Asian river known as the Menderes or Maeander (whence the verb "meander"), Daedalus fulfilled Minos's order, and the resulting structure was dubbed *Labyrinthos* (whence the noun "labyrinth"). Some years later Minos would stumble upon his craftsman's wooden cow, a discovery which put an end to Daedalus's Cretan career—for the rest of the story, *see* TO FLY TOO CLOSE TO THE SUN (p. 104).

In the meantime, the king's son traveled to Athens for the season's athletic games. The Cretan prince won these handily, provoking Athenean jealousy and a successful plot on his life. Minos's vengeance was swift, as he crushed the Greek city with his impressive war machine, relenting only when the Athenians agreed to send Crete a yearly tribute of seven youths and seven maidens. These unfortunates were then set loose in the Labyrinth, doomed to be snacks to the Minotaur.

Athens was outmatched until one day King Aegeus's long-lost son Theseus made his way to the city and established his birthright. Theseus's first act was to rid the neighborhood of the Minotaur's bovine father, which Heracles had let loose in Attica [*see* p. 114]. His second job was to get rid of the Minotaur itself, and so he volunteered to serve as one of the seven youths sent in that year's tribute to Minos.

When Theseus arrived in Crete, he caught the eye of Minos's daughter Ariadne, who fell as desperately in love with the Athenean as her mother had with the bull. Ariadne, on the promise of marriage, agreed to help her fiancé do away with the Minotaur. Like her mother, she turned to Daedalus, begging from him a clew of fine but indestructible thread,

which Theseus was to unravel as he made his way into the center of the Labyrinth. Hardly working up a sweat, Theseus butchered the monster with a charmed sword Ariadne had given him, and used Ariadne's thread to retrace his steps, bringing the Minotaur's other intended victims with him.

Their trip home, however, was rather less glorious. Though Theseus brought Ariadne along, maintaining the façade of engagement, he stopped off on an island and left without her. (Don't feel too bad—she ended up marrying the god Dionysus, who was a lot more fun than any Athenean prince.) And as Theseus sailed into the appointed Attic harbor, he forgot to raise the white sails which were to signify his success in Crete. King Aegeus, noting the ship's black sails, presumed that his son was dead, and promptly threw himself off a cliff into the sea—thenceforth known as the Aegean Sea. Theseus was sorry, but not too sorry, since his father's death meant he was now king of Athens.

Though Minos would continue to be a bother, the Atheneans eventually raised a force sufficient to reach Crete and destroy its palace—at least, that's what the Atheneans said. Archaeologists have shown that someone or something ravaged the Cretan capital Cnossos circa 1400 B.C., but this date does not jibe with the Greek fancy that Minos and Theseus lived a generation before the Trojan War (now dated to the mid-thirteenth century B.C.). In any event, Minos wasn't around to fiddle while Cnossos burned, because he himself had already been burned to death while pursuing Daedalus in Sicily—once again, *see* TO FLY TOO CLOSE TO THE SUN (p. 104).

PEGASUS

Greek myth is full of hybrid creatures—Sirens, Satyrs, the Chimera, the Sphinx, etc.—all unnatural and none of them up to much good. But Pegasus, a winged white horse, is the exception which proves the rule. To be sure, his birth was inauspicious: he sprang from the blood of Medusa, a wicked creature slain by the hero Perseus [see p. 155]. But Pegasus immediately took flight from this sad and violent world to frolic with the gods. Zeus especially delighted in the beast and allowed it to live at his palace, where Pegasus became the bearer of Zeus's lightning bolts.

Pegasus spent the rest of his time on Mount Helicon, home of the divine Muses, and one day he helped them out of a jam. The Muses had developed a rivalry with the so-called Pierides, daughters of a Macedonian king who had hubristically given them the Muses's names. Just to prove who was boss, the Muses challenged the Pierides to a singing contest, and it turned out to be no contest at all. So powerful was the Muses' song that the Helicon itself, inspired by the tune, began rising to the heavens. Poseidon, among other gods (a territorial bunch), decided things had gone too far, and so he commanded Pegasus to kick the mountain back down.

Pegasus gave the Helicon so good a kick that he punched a hole in it. Out spouted the sacred Hippocrene spring, whose waters became a source of the Muses' inspiration. This incident may explain Pegasus's name (or vice versa), which derives from the Greek for "spring." (It may otherwise refer to his springing from Medusa's blood, or, as Hesiod claims, to his birth near the fabled source of all springs.)

Pegasus also figures in the story of Bellerophon, whom, as we have seen, he helped in slaying the monstrous Chimera [*see* p. 148]. His pride puffed up, Bellerophon later attempted to fly Pegasus all the way to heaven, but either fell off in transit or was pushed. (Some say that Zeus sent down an overgrown gadfly to rile the horse.) Pegasus, however, kept on flying, ultimately taking his home in the stars as the constellation which now bears his name.

The English poet John Milton referred to this tale in his epic poem *Paradise Lost* (1667), comparing himself to Bellerophon but hoping that his lofty poetic journey would not

end in a like result. Milton alludes to the idea, dating to the fifteenth century, that Pegasus was given by the Muses especially to poets to accommodate their flights of fancy. But novelists shouldn't feel left out. Explaining his daily routine of dictating prose to a typist, the narrator of Vladimir Nabokov's *Look at the Harlequins!* (1974) notes that "We usually had a ten-minute break around four—or four-thirty if I could not rein in snorting Pegasus on the dot."

A Phoenix from the Ashes

According to the Roman historian Tacitus, a Phoenix appeared in Egypt in A.D. 35, "a remarkable event which occasioned much discussion by Egyptian and Greek authorities." Though Tacitus doesn't know what to make of the story, he duly notes that this bird was said by some to live 500 years, and by others 1461. That means we can look forward to seeing one again in the year 2035—or perhaps, granting the outside figure, 2957.

Lifespan isn't the only detail open to doubt. The Phoenix is most famous for rising from its own ashes—a pretty neat trick, no doubt, but one at variance with the earliest accounts. Herodotus, for example, reported in the fifth century B.C. only that the Phoenix carries its deceased parent to the Temple of the Sun at Heliopolis in Egypt; this happens once every 500 years. Herodotus does not know, or seem to care, how one Phoenix dies and another is born.

Later writers are much more interested in the bird's reproduction. They all agree on a few "facts": that there is only one Phoenix alive at any given time, that it resides in Ethiopia, that it resembles an eagle, and that its beautiful feathers are fire-red and golden. Beyond that, they are pleased to differ. The natural historian Pliny supposed that when the Phoenix died, a worm would crawl from its corpse. Once thoroughly baked by the African sun, this worm would be transformed into a new Phoenix. Almost as disgusting is Tacitus's version: sensing its end is near, the Phoenix builds a nest of spices, over which it spreads a coat of semen. From this nest is born

a new Phoenix, who then carries his father in this nest to Heliopolis, where the carcass is burned.

You will notice in these accounts that even if there are ashes, the Phoenix doesn't rise from them. Lucian's rendition, from the second century A.D., better suits modern fancies. In his version, the Phoenix again builds its spice nest, this time fanning its wings to help the sun ignite it, and then proceeding to self-immolate. A new Phoenix indeed "rises from the ashes," and at last we have a tale to capture the centuries' imagination. This version, which made its way into English literature circa 1400, is the one preferred by Shakespeare, who was the first to apply it metaphorically.

Today the bird is only a metaphor, but an allegedly authentic Phoenix was captured in Egypt during the reign of the Roman emperor Claudius (A.D. 41–54). Ignoring the fact that no Phoenix was scheduled to visit Egypt again until at least A.D. 535, Claudius exhibited his specimen as the real thing, hoping to convert the discovery into some much-needed P.R. Nobody, of course, took the bird seriously. I myself am withholding judgment until 2035.

THE PYTHON

If we are to credit the Greek myth, the entire clan of tropical constrictors called pythons descends from one infamous ancestor, the fabled Python. This dreaded serpent or dragon was said to have arisen from the mud left behind by the Great Flood of Deucalion [*see* p. 100]. So the Python was a kind of superworm, since worms were also once believed to breed from mud.

Some say Python arose spontaneously, others that Hera lent a hand; either way, that goddess adopted the snake as a pet and employed it in a series of unspeakable tasks. For example, she farmed out the dastardly Typhon [*see* p. 172] to the Python for lessons in wickedness. Later Hera charged her dragon to destroy Zeus's current paramour Leto, who was pregnant at the time. Zeus caught wind of the plot, however, and turned Leto into a quail, spiriting her to the island of Delos where, in human form again, she gave birth to the twin gods Apollo and Artemis.

Almost as soon as he was born, the prescient Apollo divined the Python's assignment; taking up a big bow in his

BY JOVE!

little arms he charged off to slay the beast. Mission accomplished, Apollo instituted the so-called Pythian Games, a pan-Hellenic athletic contest held annually on the spot of his conquest. (In truth, to spoil the tale, these games date only to the early sixth century B.C.) The place of Python's demise, on the southern slopes of Mount Parnassus, was itself called Pytho, though in later times it would be known as Delphi, site of Apollo's most famous temple and his medium-in-residence, called the Pythia.

In some versions of the tale, the Python too was a potent soothsayer. There are hints of an ancient Pythian snake cult involving augury, a cult suppressed upon the introduction of the newer Olympian religion—conquered by Apollo, as it were. According to later Greek interpretation, Apollo's slaying of Python represents the sun's conquest of darkness (Apollo's arrows being sunbeams). In any case, the beast was said to be buried under a rock at Apollo's oracle known as the *omphalos*, "navel," because it was thought to be the center of the world [see p. 196].

The first English references to this myth date to the late fourteenth century, when the word "pythoness" described a woman who claimed the powers of Apollo's Pythia. "Python" itself first referred to the mythical beast, and then to any familiar spirit who would possess a hapless mortal and use him as a mouthpiece. The word was not used as a name for the genus of snakes much before the 1836 edition of *The Penny Cyclopedia of the Society for the Diffusion of Useful Knowledge*, which refers to the "murderous power and voracity of the Indian boas or Pythons." By that time the older usage of "python" had disappeared, slain by the beams of science.

THE SPHINX

Wherever Hesiod learned about sphinxes (they'd already been around for several millennia), he introduced the Greek version as a deadly offspring of the Chimera. He also refers in passing to a story best known today from Sophocles' tragedy *Oedipus the King*. It seems that Hera held a grudge against Thebes because its founder, Cadmus, had the gall to be related to one of Zeus's paramours [*see* TO SOW DRAGON'S TEETH, p. 136]. To exercise her spite, Hera sent Thebes the Sphinx. This monster, perching herself on a rock outside the city, would pose an obscure riddle to each passerby, and then eat him when he failed to solve it. Thebes' tourist industry was shot.

King Creon, at his wits' end, sought out the advice of an oracle. Assured that the Sphinx would kill herself if anyone cracked one of her riddles, Creon offered his crown and the hand of his sister Jocasta to whoever could outwit the monster. The lucky winner turned out to be a visitor from Corinth named Oedipus, who answered this question: "What animal goes on four legs in the morning, two at noon, and three in the evening?" (The answer is "man.") The Sphinx promptly threw herself off the rock, and Oedipus returned to Thebes to claim his prizes—only later discovering that he wasn't so lucky after all, since Jocasta was in fact his mother.

It is possible that the Greeks inherited some form of this legend from Egypt, where sphinxes were native. But the sphinxes of Greek art are based on Assyrian models, which were winged and female; the Egyptian variety were wingless and male, being in fact portrait statues of pharaohs, with the king's head stuck on a lion's body. At least, that's what they had become by the reign of the pharaoh Khafre (circa 2550 B.C.), whose head adorns the famous Great Sphinx at Giza. Recently, geologists associated with Boston University have suggested that Khafre merely restored a sphinx which had first been carved sometime before 5000 B.C.

It's appropriate that the riddling Sphinx should remain shrouded in mystery, especially since she is better known in English literature for her obscure wisdom than for her monstrous appetite. Shakespeare's character Berowne even goes so far as to call love "Subtle [clever] as Sphinx," thinking that some sort of praise. "Sphinx-like," meaning "riddling," "mysterious," "poker-faced," remains vaguely complimentary, though sometimes in a hostile way; nobody likes a know-it-all.

A SOP TO CERBERUS

It is said that the ancient Egyptians used fierce dogs to guard their graves; if so, this practice may have inspired the Greek myth of Cerberus, Hades' favorite pet. Hesiod describes Cerberus, one of Typhon's monstrous brood, as a fearsome canine with fifty heads, a number later writers reduced to three. But they also gave Cerberus the tail of a serpent and a mane of snakes, making it difficult to say which version is more hideous.

Hades chained Cerberus up on the underworld side of the river Styx, the point of no return for shades of the dead. Cerberus's job was to see that no living person trespassed on Hades' grounds and that no shade departed—anyone trying would be eaten. On occasion, however, one hero or another found it necessary to visit a famous shade and would have to devise some way of getting past that dog.

One such hero was Aeneas, the leading man in Virgil's Latin epic the *Aeneid*. According to Virgil, Aeneas crosses the Styx in the company of a prophetess called the Sibyl, who has come prepared for Cerberus. As they land on the nether shore, they spy the monster glaring out of a cave, his snaky neck bristling. The Sibyl quickly pulls out a honeyed wheat cake and tosses it to Cerberus, who's apparently been starved to sharpen his appetite for would-be escapees. Included in the Sibyl's recipe is a sleeping potion, so after the dog gobbles her cake it promptly rolls over in a doze.

From this and similar stories comes the expression "a sop to Cerberus," meaning "an appeasement" or "a bribe," especially when the party to be appeased has a Cerberus-like disposition. A "sop" isn't a cake exactly, but a dipping bread soaked in wine, milk, or some other liquid (whence our expressions "to sop up" and "milksop"). This food, if you could call it that, was apparently more familiar than cakes to sixteenth-century Britons, and so when the Scotsman Gavin Douglas first translated the *Aeneid* into English in 1513, he described the Sibyl's gift as "a sop steeped in honey." This translation has yielded not only the phrase "a sop to Cerberus," but also the expression "to throw someone a sop," and in turn our use of "sop" in the sense of "bribe."

A TYPHOON

The etymology of "typhoon" is one big mess, as no fewer than three different foreign words influenced its development, spelling, and usage. The oldest spelling (dating to the late sixteenth century) is "touffon," from the ancient Urdu noun *tufan*, "a tempest, a hurricane." By the early nineteenth century, however, others were spelling the word "Tay-fun" and "Ty-foong," both somewhat odd-looking attempts to render the Chinese *tai fung*, "big wind." It is from this latter spelling that "typhoon" eventually emerged, but only by way of association with an ancient mythological troublemaker named Typhon.

According to Hesiod, Typhon (a.k.a. Typhoeus), a son of Gaia and Tartarus, was a terrible dragon with one hundred serpents' heads and many mighty hands and feet. He was able not only to mimic godly speech and beastly howling, but also to shoot fire from his brows. Typhon was so evil and deadly, in fact, that even the gods cowered, fleeing to Egypt disguised as animals.

After he could no longer stand Athena's ridicule, Zeus decided to fight back, grabbing an armful of lightning bolts and pitching them dragon-ward. This prompted Typhon to fight fire with fire. The exchange was so fierce that Mother Earth began to melt, the seas were set a-boiling, and the whole planet would have been fried to a crisp if Zeus hadn't swept down from Olympus to scorch off all Typhon's heads with one well-aimed bolt.

As you can imagine, Typhon didn't have much fight left in him after that; Zeus handily hurled him, or what was left of him, down into the bosom of his father Tartarus. Typhon wasn't quite through making trouble, though deprived of his fire he was reduced to stirring up sea storms. He also spawned a number of children capable of causing various Greek heroes a pain in the posterior, namely Cerberus, Hydra, and Orthrus [see pp. 170, 111, 116].

The association of Typhon with destructive tempests guided the English rendering of *tai fung* as "typhoon," even though Typhon could not have caused typhoons anywhere near Greece. (The word is properly applied only to storms in the western Pacific and the Chinese Sea.) But, to complicate matters further, it is possible that Typhon in fact took his name from some cognate of the Urdu *tufan*, since the monster was apparently a Near-Eastern export. Indeed, many Asian myths refer to a storm-god's ascendancy over the heavens after conquering a horrible sea monster. The Phoenician storm-god Baal, for example, uses two clubs fashioned by his favored artisans (compare the Cyclopes) to bludgeon the unruly Yamm ("Sea"), and/or a seven-headed terror named Lotan.

This Phoenician tale finds echoes not only in Greek myth but also in the Biblical account of Leviathan (a name perhaps related to Lotan's). "Thou [God] brakest the heads of the dragons in the waters," says the Psalmist. "Thou brakest the heads of leviathan in pieces, and gavest him to be meat to the people inhabiting the wilderness" (Psalms 74:13–14). The Greeks may have wished the same fate on Typhon, who, while his heads were broken, continued to make mincemeat of Greek sailors.

CHARMED OBJECTS, MAGICAL PLACES, AND BIZARRE STATES OF BEING

AMBROSIA AND NECTAR

"Ambrosia" now refers to any especially tasty or sweet-smelling stuff (in particular a type of sticky almond candy) and to an entire genus of ironically tasteless ragweeds. The Greeks, however, had something more dignified in mind: "ambrosia," deriving from the Greek for "immortal," was the food of their gods. Both ambrosia and the drink used to wash it down, called "nectar" (perhaps based on the Greek for "death"), conferred immortality and prevented wear and tear on the body. Thus the goddess Thetis, in Homer's *Iliad* (Book 19), embalms the corpse of the hero Patroclus by smearing it with ambrosia and nectar.

The two words first appear in English in direct reference to Greek mythology, which had become a hot topic again by the sixteenth century. "It is for gods," says Montaigne in John Florio's 1603 translation, "to mount wing'd horses, and to feed on Ambrosia." Within a century, however, the words were separated from myth and began serving as general names for heavenly comestibles.

The Greeks themselves were not entirely clear on the recipes for nectar and ambrosia, or even on which was the food and which the drink. Yet both seem to have been thought of as super versions of honey, one of the Greeks' true passions. So "ambrosia" naturally became in later times a synonym for beebread, the pollen and nectar compound bees feed to their young.

An Apple of Discord

The Judgment of Paris · The Trojan War

An "apple of discord" is essentially the same thing as a "bone of contention," only more dignified. You might even call it glamorous, since the phrase ultimately derives from a mythological beauty contest.

The story begins at the wedding of the hero Peleus and the water-nymph Thetis, parents of the famous Achilles. All the gods were invited to the party, saving one: Eris, goddess of discord—an understandable omission. Eris, however, didn't see it that way and resolved to get revenge.

Her clever scheme was to steal one of Hera's golden apples—which had themselves been a wedding gift [see THE GARDEN OF THE HESPERIDES, p. 190]—and inscribe it "Property of the Fairest." Eris then tossed this vanity grenade onto a banquet table, where it was squabbled over by every goddess on hand. The field was eventually narrowed to the three

proudest and most powerful ones—Hera, Aphrodite, and Athena—and Zeus was called upon to settle the dispute.

Zeus must have been mighty tempted to award the apple to his wife—if only to keep her out of his hair for a while—but the last thing he needed was the wrath of Aphrodite and Athena. So he packed the trio off with Hermes to Mount Ida (near Troy), where they would find his appointed judge, Paris, a handsome guy in his own right.

Finding himself unable to decide the case on its merits, Paris opened the floor to bids. Hera tempted Paris with rule over Asia, Athena promised him military glory, and Aphrodite offered the hand of the world's most beautiful woman. Appropriately enough, Paris traded beauty for beauty, and equally appropriately the resulting marriage spawned more discord than anybody but Eris could have imagined. Paris's new wife was the Greek queen Helen of Sparta, who, unfortunately, was already espoused to King Menelaus. When Paris returned home to Troy with his prize and was recognized as the long-lost son of King Priam, a major to-do between Greece and Troy was assured. We call it the Trojan War.

All this from one little golden apple, and so "apple of discord" most properly signifies a prize not worth the commotion it causes. Early versions of the phrase, such as "apple of dissension" and "apple of contention," were in use by the seventeenth century, but the current form does not appear to have been used before the nineteenth.

ATLANTIS

Lord knows the Greeks were confused when it came to deciding just who and what lay west of the known world. Things were bad enough with Elysium, the Fortunate Isles, and the Garden of the Hesperides to contend with. But then someone cooked up another occidental paradise called Atlantis, which caused etymological as well as geographical problems.

Tales of Atlantis may have begun circulating in Greece in about the sixth century B.C., but if so they amounted to little until Plato concocted a detailed picture in his fourth-century dialogues *Timaeus* and *Critias*. Plato's Atlantis was a great island once situated in the Atlantic just beyond the Pillars of Hercules. Larger than Libya and Asia put together, Atlantis was arranged in three rings of land separated by two rings of water and bounded by the ocean. This curious arrangement was engineered by the god Poseidon, who appointed as king his eldest son Atlas, born along with nine brothers to the mortal Clito, whose own parents had been the island's original inhabitants.

Plato says that Atlantis was named after this Atlas, who himself must have been named after the one who held up the sky [see p. 14]. Not only was the island supposed to be located near Mount Atlas, but a towering mountain also stood at its center. And though Plato claims the Atlantic Ocean was named after the island, in truth the island was probably named after the ocean, which itself was probably named after the original Atlas. Nobody ever said these myths weren't confounding.

In any case, Atlas and his successors ruled wisely over a place of great beauty and wealth, turning it into a utopia of reason and law. The Atlanteans were also well-trained warriors, and in time they managed to invade and subdue the western mainlands of Europe and Africa. But as the immortal element thinned in the Atlanteans' blood, they grew more covetous and less reasonable. As a result they waged an unwise campaign to subdue Greece itself, only to be decisively beaten by a much smaller army of Athenians. (Plato claims that this great battle took place in the ninety-fourth century B.C.)

Eventually driven off the European and African mainlands as well, the Atlanteans retreated home to suffer further degeneration. After a time the gods could no longer bear their wickedness, so Poseidon caused the ocean to swallow up the island in a day. This part of the story may be based on some actual cataclysm, perhaps the submerging of an island in the Mediterranean after a traumatic volcanic eruption. (Archaeologists once suggested the island Thira, a Minoan settlement, about 70 miles from Crete, temporarily engulfed by the sea circa 1500 B.C.) The rest is sheer fantasy, which Plato himself hardly took seriously—he was more interested in reforming Athens than in raising Atlantis.

A Cornucopia

The etymology of "cornucopia" is very straightforward: it's from the Latin *cornu copia* (or *copiae*), "horn of plenty." But, as you might expect, the myth behind it is a cornucopia of conflicting details.

One version of the horn-of-plenty tale begins when Zeus is born, out of his father Cronus's sight, on the island of Crete [*see* TITANIC, p. 6]. His mother, Rhea, entrusts the godling to the daughters of King Melisseus, one of whom, Amalthea, feeds him his daily goat's milk. In between servings she hides Zeus in a tree, were Cronus (who periodically scans the earth for signs of trouble) can't see him.

When Zeus is old enough to lead his rebellion against the Titans, he cloaks himself with the skin of the goat that had nourished him. Victorious, the god brings this goat (none the worse for skinning) up to Mount Olympus as a special pet; but one day he accidently snaps off one of its horns. Recalling Amalthea's kindness, he presents her with the horn, now rigged to fill itself up with whatever fruits she desires. Amalthea's horn was thus a horn of unending plenty, a *cornu copia*.

There are other versions of the tale. In one, Amalthea is, rather than a nymph, the goat itself, which as a reward for its service is placed in the heavens as a constellation minus one horn; this plenteous appendage is then given to the daughters of King Melisseus. In yet another version, the river-god Achelous takes on the shape of a bull in order to battle Heracles, to whom he loses a horn. Depending on whom you believe at this point, either some river-nymphs fill this horn with flowers and fruits, whence it becomes a horn of plenty, or the smarting Achelous borrows Amalthea's horn to trade to Heracles for the horn he's lost.

Wherever the darn thing came from, the cornucopia is first mentioned in extant English texts in 1592 by Robert Greene, who represents it as gripped in Hospitality's fist. Soon after, it shows up in the translators' preface to the King James Version of the Bible (1611): "Men talk of Cornu-copia, that it had all things necessary for food in it." At about the same time, "cornucopia" took on figurative dimensions, and began to be used as a metaphorical term for anything especially bountiful, which is the only way it is used today.

A CYNOSURE

Amalthea didn't grab all the glory for babysitting the young Zeus on Crete [*see* A CORNUCOPIA, p. 182]. Another Cretan nymph, named Cynosura, was rewarded after Zeus's conquest of the Titans by being transformed into a star and placed in a brilliant constellation. The Greeks thought this a very high honor indeed, especially since Cynosura's constellation, appearing fixed in the night sky, helped guide navigators.

Skeptical? I don't blame you, and in this case etymology is on your side. The Greek *cynosura*, meaning "dog's tail," is an unlikely name for a nymph but a relatively appropriate one for the constellation Ursa Minor, which reminded ancient stargazers of that canine appendage. Perhaps the star they called Cynosura, around which the others appear to revolve and which we now call Polaris or the North Star, was a glorified nymph whose name is lost, but if I were she I'd be a little insulted to be compared to a dog's posterior.

In any case, "cynosure" was adopted into English late in the sixteenth century as a nickname for the North Star or for the entire constellation of Ursa Minor. Since Polaris is so important and reliable a guide, "cynosure" took on the connotations "a guiding light" and then "a center of attention." The latter is the principal meaning today.

THE ELYSIAN FIELDS AND FORTUNATE ISLES

Parisians may fancy their city a modern-day Elysium, and their Champs-Elysées its Elysian fields, but you may have a different vision of paradise—particularly if you don't speak French.

Besides, the Greeks knew that Elysium was a place few of them would ever see, especially since postcards weren't available. A mythical paradise where the Golden Age lived on, Elysium lay beyond the ocean and the bounds of the known world. According to Homer, it was a place reserved for heroes, sent there by the gods to escape death. (There was once only a thin line between heroism and godhood.) Once in Elysium, these heroes were free to frolic on the beautiful fields under a sun that never set.

This happy picture would not remain so simple once the Greeks started thinking harder about it. Hesiod threw a wrench in the works by portraying a distinctly Elysian place called the Isles of the Blessed, *Fortunatae Insulae* in Latin and so more familiarly the "Fortunate Isles" in English. These islands, thought to be somewhat closer than Elysium, were reserved for the heroes of Hesiod's fourth age, which he called the Heroic Age—the time of the great war between Greece and Troy.

Since Hesiod's description of the Fortunate Isles was both similar to and different from Homer's description of Elysium, later Greeks weren't sure whether they were the same place or not. Eventually most came to believe that Elysium was a temporary resting place in the underworld for the shades of good men before their reincarnation on earth. If a man managed to life three virtuous lives, his shade could then retire to the Fortunate Isles for an eternity of fun and games. This notion was consistent with their vague belief in immortality and also with their growing skepticism that even heroes could escape death.

The location of Elysium was settled, but that of the Fortunate Isles was not. The Roman natural historian Pliny the Elder supposed they were identical to the Canary Islands, off the western coast of Africa; the historian Plutarch, on the other hand, improbably believed they were at the center of the earth; while the philosopher Lucian put them near to the moon. Nobody suggested that either the Fortunate Isles or Elysium was in France.

ENTHUSIASM

Once you realize what it means, you might lose your zeal for enthusiasm. The Greek word *enthousiasmos*, "inspiration," literally means "full of the god," which I suppose could be interesting, but knowing the Greek gods I think I'd rather not.

For their part, the Greeks regarded *enthousiasmos* as something of a holy state. Any number of poets and philosophers—including Socrates—would brag of their enthusiasm, thus implying that their work was approved by the gods. (To style yourself *enthousiasmos* was sort of like attaching "Ph.D." to your name.) By this means poets sometimes promoted themselves as prophets, as *enthousiasmos* also referred to the possession of a medium by a god or demon, usually resulting in bizarre ranting and wild gesturing.

The English rendering was originally true to its Greek roots; it first appeared in Philemon Holland's 1603 translation of Plutarch's *Moralia*, where it is said that "demons use to make their prophets and prophetesses to be ravished with an Enthusiasm or divine fury." As spiritual possession came to seem mere superstition, "enthusiasm" gradually took on new meaning, referring to a fervor which stems not from divine inspiration but from intense personal feeling. The sense "great appetite or passion"—as in "an enthusiasm for heavy metal"—is a twentieth-century development.

FASCINATION

One of the best-known clichés in ancient Greece was "speak no evil of the dead." Common courtesy aside, the Greeks believed malicious words wounded the shades of the departed, provoking them to seek revenge.

Furthermore, speaking evil, whether of the dead or of the living, was tantamount to wishing it, and such wishes were considered especially powerful. From the Greek word for such evil-speaking—*baskainein* (to slander, bewitch, cast the evil eye)—the Romans fashioned an equivalent: *fascinare* (from *fari*, to speak, curse, enchant). Thus to be "fascinated" (*fascinatum*) was to be bewitched.

Not very fascinating, until you discover that the word for "charm," *fascinum*, was also the Latin for "penis." Most likely the latter meaning derives from the former, in the sense "a source of potency"; but it may also have something to do with an obscure minor god named Fascinus, a phallic deity attributed with the power to counteract evil spells. To protect themselves from being *fascinati*, Romans took to wearing phallic amulets; they would even put such charms on the necks of their cows.

Dramatist Ben Jonson was the first to use "fascinate" in English, in his comedy *Every Man in His Humor* (1598), and he proves his familiarity with Latin. The braggart Bobadilla, having been soundly thrashed by an irate townsman, excuses his cowardice as the result of bewitchment: "I was fascinated, by Jupiter, fascinated; but I will be unwitch'd, and reveng'd by law." By the mid-seventeenth century, "to fascinate" had taken on the broader meaning "to enslave someone's faculties," and by the mid-nineteenth "to captivate or attract." Simultaneously, the various synonyms of "fascinate" also evolved into metaphors, so that today we can use "fascinating," "charming," "bewitching," and "spellbinding" almost interchangeably, and with equally little regard to the ancient Greeks' and Romans' sensibilities. It may be a compliment to be called "fascinating" or "charming," but if a Roman had pointed a little phallic amulet at you, it wouldn't have been because he desired your company.

THE GARDEN OF THE HESPERIDES

Once upon a time, Zeus ordered three ladies named the Hesperides—nymphs of sleep—to guard some apple trees that Gaia (the Earth) had given his wife Hera as a wedding gift. These were no ordinary trees: the apples they bore were golden. And the place they grew—situated near Mount Atlas and called the "Garden of the Hesperides"—was no ordinary place: among the fabulous fruits of its soil was the divine ambrosia [see p. 177]. Such a magical garden would of course be a magnet for thieves, so Zeus gave the sleepy Hesperides a little helper named Ladon, a cave-dwelling serpent or dragon with (some claim) a hundred heads.

This beast was not altogether effective, since he left unmolested some brigands sent by one of the neighboring tyrants. By some accounts it was left to Heracles to rescue the Hesperides, a good deed that prompted their father Atlas to award him the golden apples he'd come looking for [see p. 166], though Heracles was forced to support the heavens while Atlas fetched them. Others say that Heracles had to steal his prize, and slay Ladon to do so. Whichever way you like, the tale of Heracles and the golden apples seems related to his gradual transformation from a hero into a god, since the apples, besides being precious, were reputedly a source of immortality.

There is much unresolved speculation about the source of this strange myth. Perchance the Hesperides were originally peoples of western Africa whose claim to fame was their immense flocks of sheep (the Greek word for "sheep" also means "apple"). It is in any case likely that the tale incorporates the vestigial notion that a paradise flourished at the edge of the world, since it was supposed that the garden was situated near the so-called Fortunate Isles [*see* p. 185]. If so, then the Garden of the Hesperides was the Greeks' Eden and Ladon its serpent, with Heracles fulfilling here, to complete the parallel, the role of God's avenging son.

THE GOLDEN FLEECE

JASON AND THE ARGONAUTS · MEDEA
THE HELLESPONT

I first read of the Golden Fleece in a comic book starring Walt Disney's inimitable skinflint, Scrooge McDuck. Uncle Scrooge, ever eager to stuff his vault with more fabulous and priceless objects, enlisted his nephew Donald Duck, plus his great-nephews Huey, Dewey, and Louie, in this latest quest for fool's gold. All Scrooge cared about, of course, was the fleece's value in U.S. dollars, but if he'd brushed up his mythology he'd have realized that gold meant nothing to the fleece's original seekers, Jason and his Argonauts.

The legend of the Golden Fleece was probably simple at first, but as with the tales of Heracles' labors and Odysseus's odyssey, it would become a frame into which the Greeks packed dozens of elaborate, if tangential, adventures. Most of these will not detain us, but here are the essentials:

The story begins with a jealous stepmother, namely Ino, daughter of Cadmus and second wife of King Athamas of Thebes. Ino came, as story-book stepmothers will, to despise Athamas's children, whom she aimed to bump off so that her own brood might inherit the throne. But the intended victims, Phrixus and Helle, catching wind of the plot, availed themselves of a certain ram Hermes had given the city, and which had a golden fleece, wings, and the power of speech. Phrixus and Helle secured business-class seats on ram, which then took off in the general direction of the Black Sea.

Unfortunately, Helle forgot her bottle of Halcion, and, growing dizzy, fell off the ram into the strait between the Aegean Sea and the Sea of Marmara; this strait would thenceforth be known as the "Hellespont." Her brother Phrixus, however, touched down safely in the kingdom of Colchis, at the far eastern end of the Black Sea. He rewarded the ram by sacrificing it to Zeus on the spot, while the local ruler, King Aeëtes, believing the ram's fleece to be charmed, suspended it from a tree in a grove sacred to the god Ares, setting a guard dragon beneath it.

Meanwhile back in Greece, more family conflict arose in the Thessalian kingdom of Iolcus, as the rightful ruler, Aeson, was dispossessed of the throne by his wicked half-brother Pelias. Aeson, being old and feeble, could do little on his own behalf, but his son Jason was more vigorous, so Pelias attempted in various ways to be rid of him. Pelias finally hit on the plan of promising Jason the throne if the latter could recover the Golden Fleece. (Pelias wasn't very imaginative—*compare* A CHIMERA, p. 148, *and* MEDUSA'S HEAD, p. 155.) Having no idea of what he was up against, Jason agreed to the deal, and he immediately instructed the craftsman Argus to build a great ship for the purpose. The result, called the *Argo* after its architect, could accommodate fifty oarsmen and was the first ship of its kind ever built.

After Jason had signed up a crew, which included virtually every hero of the day (Heracles, Theseus, Orpheus, Castor, Pollux, et al.), they set out on their merry way and had many a thrilling adventure. Eventually Jason and the so-called Argonauts reached Colchis and made King Aeëtes an offer he couldn't refuse. Aeëtes did attach some strings to the fleece; first, Jason would have to yoke two fire-breathing oxen to a huge plow and sow the dragon's teeth left over from Cadmus's Boeotian adventure [*see* p. 136]. When these teeth yielded a crop of fearsome warriors, Jason would have to single-handedly dispatch them. When that was done he could help himself to the Golden Fleece—provided, of course, he could get past the dragon guarding it.

Jason would have been dead meat had Aeëtes' daughter Medea not fallen in love with him. Medea, who was well versed in magical arts, promised Jason her help on the condition that he marry her and take her back to Greece—life with Aeëtes was apparently no picnic. By this point, Jason was well used to conditions, so he promised Medea his hand, and thus the sorceress guided him through each dangerous step in the fleece's recovery. She advised him, for example, that he could never kill the warriors born of the dragon's teeth, and that he should, like Cadmus, merely throw a stone among them, which would cause them to kill each other. She also charmed the dragon to sleep, making it simple for Jason to remove the fleece from its tree.

Anticipating that Aeëtes might renege on the deal, especially now that Medea had switched sides, the Argonauts set sail under cover of darkness. Aeëtes, however, followed in hot pursuit. Medea had the foresight to bring her young brother along in the *Argo*, and to slow her father's pursuit she chopped the boy up and threw the pieces into the water. As expected, Aeëtes gave up the chase in order to collect his sons' remains, but by any measure Medea had made a bad move. Not only was Aeëtes all the more bent on revenge, but Zeus also got hot under the collar when he heard of her despicable crime. Aeëtes sent a whole fleet after the *Argo*, and Zeus pestered the ship with a series of terrifying and relentless storms.

The *Argo*, after taking all the punishment it could stand, finally piped up, informing the Argonauts that Zeus would never relent until they had been purified by Medea's aunt, the witch Circe, whose island lay way out west in the Ocean. Though it meant taking a long detour, Jason really had no choice, so he posted off to Circe's island for absolution. But this was not the end of the Argonauts' troubles, as they were forced, on the way back to Thessaly, to run a gauntlet of monsters—terrible creatures such as the Sirens and Scylla and Charybdis, most of them better known from Homer's *Odyssey* and from my previous book, *It's Greek to Me!*

After evading a rather tiresome series of perils, Jason, Medea, and the Argonauts finally reached Iolcus with the fleece; predictably enough, Pelias was *not* glad to see them. The talented Medea, however, disposed of that problem, persuading Pelias's gullible daughters to boil their father to death in a big pot. She would also go on to dispose of her own sons by Jason, along with her husband's new lover, good deeds that earned her exile to Athens.

As for Jason, some say that he committed suicide out of grief for his sons and lover. Others relate the more poetically just tale that as Jason lay resting in the shade beneath the *Argo*, a piece of the ship's poop fell off and crushed him to death. What happened to the Golden Fleece, though, is a mystery; perhaps Scrooge McDuck knows the answer.

THE ORACLE AT DELPHI

Ancient divination was hardly restricted to such crude devices as bird-watching and entrail-reading [*see* UNDER THE AUSPICES, p. 205]. More sophisticated and direct was the consulting of oracles (*manteia* in Greek)—responses of a god to particular questions. Such oracles did not come straight from the horse's mouth, however. They required a bureaucracy of intermediaries, including a medium who channeled the god's response and a host of prophets to interpret it.

Though not the oldest of *manteia* (which also referred to the places such prophecies were given), the oracle at Delphi was preeminent. Originally called Pytho [*see* p. 166], Delphi was sacred to the god Apollo, an infallible prognosticator who deigned to answer seekers' questions in return for valuable offerings. Apollo's medium was herself called "the Pythia," and in order to channel the god she would work herself into a divine fury (perhaps with the help of certain foul-smelling narcotic gasses). Perched upon her tripod, she would rant for the benefit of the sacred interpreters, who converted the prophecy into lines of verse and presented them to the grateful seeker.

The seeker, however, had no cause to be *too* grateful, since these verses were often quite ambiguous if not impenetrable—their obscurity perhaps being intended to protect the god when a prophecy turned out false. From the ambiguity of Apollo's oracles we derive two English words: "delphic" and "oracular" (*oracula* was the Romans' equivalent of *manteia*). Both now mean "mysterious and inscrutable, if pretentious," though at first "oracular" meant "divinely inspired" or "infallible." Only skepticism has made the two words synonyms.

Through the fog of obfuscation, the Delphic oracle was still a source of high moral teaching, being especially concerned with petitioners' character and intentions. Carved on the walls of Apollo's temple, furthermore, were some of the hoariest pieces of ancient ethics, such as "Nothing in excess" and "Know thyself." The oracle also gave political counsel, generally conservative in nature and favoring those in power; but, oddly enough, it also seemed to welcome various foreign invasions, for example the failed attempts of Croesus of Lydia and of the Persians, as well as the successful one of Philip of Macedon. It probably didn't hurt the invaders' causes that they, Croesus in particular, contributed greatly to the temple's store of treasures.

The Delphic oracle's authority in the Greek world had much to do with Apollo's reputation and with the quality and professionalism of the service; but it also had to do with the belief that Delphi, located on a slope of Mount Parnassus, was the exact center of the world. This "fact" had supposedly been revealed when Zeus one day set one eagle at the western edge of the world and one at the eastern, releasing them at the same moment and causing them to fly at the same speed; they reportedly met at Delphi. On the spot was placed a certain stone called the *omphalos* (Greek for "navel"), various replicas of which took its place through the ages.

As for the temple itself, it also had to be replicated or restored on several occasions, when a natural disaster or attack had damaged it. (Its store of donated treasures made it a perpetual object of plunder—the Roman emperor Nero, for example, carted off 500 bronze statues.) Through it all, the oracle at Delphi continued to do business, until late in the days of the Roman Empire, when it was shut down by the Christian emperor Theodosius the Great in A.D. 390. Already by that time, however, prognostication by oracle had come to be overshadowed by a new and better method of divination, namely astrology.

THE RIVER STYX

It's only appropriate that the baneful pomp-rock band Styx should take its name from a poisonous river. Sometimes personified in Greek myth as the eldest daughter of the Titans Oceanus and Tethys, the Styx ran around the underworld in seven circles, or nine if you believe Virgil. (Dante did, which is why there are nine circles in his Inferno.)

Derived from the Greek *stygeo*, "to hate," the Styx was hateful indeed to mortals, whose shades were ushered across it into the land of death by the ferryman Charon. Styx, as Hate personified, even frightened the gods, despite her being among the first to enlist in Zeus's cause against their parents [see TITANIC, p. 6]. The story is that, as a reward, Zeus adopted Styx's children and built her a great palace in the underworld; he then charmed her waters, by which all the gods would be forced to take their oaths.

According to Hesiod, whenever an argument arose among the gods, Zeus commanded the rainbow-goddess Iris to fetch some Stygian water in a golden pot. The contending parties were then compelled to state their cases while pouring a libation, and if anyone perjured himself his punishment was hateful at best. First, he was confined to his bed for a year and prevented both from breathing and from partaking of the immortal-making substances ambrosia and nectar [see p. 177]. Then he was condemned to nine years of hard labor, and was barred from the gods' dinner parties. Needless to say, the immortals did not often swear in vain.

The Greeks identified the mythical river Styx with an actual stream in the Arcadian region which sprang from a high rock and then disappeared underground. Various superstitions were then attached to it; its waters were thought poisonous to men and animals alike, and were said to shatter iron and break pottery. On the other hand, the Styx worked wonders for the Greek hero Achilles, whose mother rendered him invulnerable—almost—by dunking him in its waters [*see* AN ACHILLES' HEEL, p. 93]. Alexander the Great, however, who fancied himself a latter-day Achilles, wasn't so lucky; by one account he tested his mettle by sipping from the stream, only to contract a dire case of water-poisoning. Perhaps this explains the fever that killed him at the age of thirty-two.

TRIVIAL

Once upon a time, "trivial" meant "beneath notice" or "inconsequential"—but that was before people started noticing what was beneath notice in order to beat friends at parlor games. It's already strange that "trivia" has become something of a compliment—not to mention a selling point for books like this one; even stranger is the fact that in Latin *trivia* roughly refers to "three roads" or "three ways." Herein lies a tale, in which you will discover the respectable Greek origins of the trivial.

One of the more mysterious Greek deities was named Hecate, a goddess of women also associated with ghosts, spirits, and other creepy things. Hecate would often pass the time wandering through the countryside frightening innocent travelers, and she haunted crossroads in particular. In ancient times your typical crossroad was what we now call a three-way or "T" intersection, *triodos* in Greek and *trivium* in Latin. To keep Hecate (nicknamed Trivia) happy, people would often post little statues at these intersections, representing the goddess with three faces or three bodies.

These statues and the offerings made at them were so effective, people thought no place could be better for an afternoon chat. Loiterers and travelers alike would meet at such crossroads to talk about all sorts of inconsequential business, which itself came to be known, after the goddess, as *trivia*. By the late sixteenth century, Englishmen had adopted this usage: "trivial" meant "commonplace" or—as used by Shakespeare—"trifling."

The word "trivia" itself, however, did not appear in English until 1908, and people didn't play "trivia games" until the 1960s. The singular "trivium," on the other hand, is of venerable age, having been the collective name for the three so-called liberal arts of grammar, logic, and rhetoric when such things were still taught in grammar schools.

UNDER THE AEGIS

Though we use "under the aegis" to mean "under the sponsorship or protection," what it really means is altogether less cozy: "under the storm cloud."

From the Greek *aisso*, "to rush or move violently," *aigis* was the name given to Zeus's shield, with which the god would thrash and storm about, causing Greeks to quake in their boots. Made to order in the image of a thundercloud by the fire-god Hephaestus, this aegis, according to Homer, was indestructible. It was also an awful thing to behold, whether wielded by Zeus or by his daughter Athena, the only god granted borrowing privileges. Garlanded with Terror, Hatred, Battle-strength, and Onslaught (Zeus's pet snakes), the shield had Medusa's head set smack in its middle—an aegis-warming gift to Athena from the hero Perseus [*see* p. 155].

As it happens, the word *aigis* also recalls the Greek *aix*, "goat," a pun that later gave rise to the contrary tale that Zeus's aegis was in fact the goatskin in which he clad himself before storming the heavens to topple his father [*see* A CORNUCOPIA, p. 182]. Forgetting all about the original, Greek artists and writers began to represent the aegis as a short goatskin cloak worn over the shoulders or on the left arm.

Over time the original aegis only sank deeper into the mists of fiction. In his 1706 tragedy *Ulysses*, Nicholas Rowe, self-consciously faithful to Homer, was the first to use "aegis" in English, describing Athena, with fair accuracy, as "shak[ing] her dreadful Aegis from the clouds." But by the end of the century the aegis was thought of less as a weapon of terror than as a cloak of protection whose power could be shed on those beneath it. Thus "aegis" became a metaphor for "defense" or "protection"—as in the eighteenth-century Swiss phrenologist J. K. Lavater's one-liner, "Feeling is the aegis of enthusiasts and fools."

The phrase "under the aegis" itself traces to an entry in the 1910 edition of *Encyclopaedia Britannica*, where reference is made to rules established "under the aegis of the Billiard Association." By this point, "aegis" had come to mean something more like "sponsorship" or "approval" than "protection." Thus "under the aegis" has become virtually synonymous with "under the auspices," though one would think storm clouds are anathema to bird-watchers.

UNDER THE AUSPICES

AUGURY · SINISTER

Today, bird-watching is a hobby; in ancient times, it was virtually a necessity. As you should appreciate by now, the Greek and Roman gods were an irritable and fickle bunch. If Zeus and Hera were squabbling, or if Venus got up on the wrong side of bed, puny mortals could be assured of rough times. And since these deities did not always deign to post notices of how they were feeling, the ancients developed various rituals for discerning the gods' dispositions.

The dust of history lies thick upon most such practices—axinomancy, for example, and aleuromancy (divination from axes and flour, respectively, when heated in sacrificial fires). But people are still known to stake their futures on the roll of a die (astragalomancy), and occasionally to seek out prophecies by randomly opening a book (bibliomancy). We recall one particular ritual whenever we use the phrase "under the auspices," which originally referred to the observation of birds. ("Auspice" is from a Latin compound of *avis*, "bird," and *spectare*, "to behold," "to inspect.")

One of the oldest methods for divining the gods' will, bird-watching was especially popular among the Romans, who established a college of so-called *Augures* (whence our word "augury") charged with interpreting all sorts of heavenly signs. Propitious signs would appear in the east, and gloomy ones in the west—left and right, respectively, to the Roman augurs, who faced south for inspection. Greek augurs, on the other hand, faced north, meaning that bad news came from the left—*sinister* in Latin. From the Greek position and the Latin adjective would arise the English "sinister."

The *Augures* did not limit themselves to auspices, but that was the bulk of their business, and in addition to keeping their eyes peeled for random sightings they would occasionally haul out a sacred chicken for scrutiny. The Romans were even known to bring such a chicken onto the field of battle, just in case they began to doubt that the gods were really on their side.

The English word "auspices" originally meant exactly what it meant to the Romans, since it first appeared in a 1533 translation of Livy. But within a century it was used metaphorically for any especially happy ("auspicious") sign or propitious influence, and in particular for a patron's good guidance. The phrase "under the auspices" itself seems to have first been used by Edmund Burke in his *Reflections on the Revolution in France* (1790): "The whole has been done under the auspices . . . of religion and piety."

MYTHOLOGICAL
LISTS

DAYS AND MONTHS

The seven-day week to which we're now so enslaved was actually a latecomer to Europe, as the ancient Greeks and Romans had no concept of a week at all. (There were a few special days in the Roman month—the Ides, for example—but there was no regular subdivision.) We have adopted this week, rather, from the ancient Egyptians, who based its length on the belief that the earth had seven "planets" revolving around it.

The most distant of these planets was the one the Romans would call Saturn, after the old harvest god and the eldest of their great deities. The other six, in order of distance, they called Jupiter, Mars, Sol (the sun), Venus, Mercury, and Luna (the moon). According to the Egyptians, each of these planets, in rotating order, governed the hours, and the planet governing the first hour of the day lent its name to it. Using the Latin nomenclature, if Saturn governed the first hour of the day, which was thus Saturn's day, Jupiter governed the second hour, Mars the third, Sol the fourth, and so on.

As the second day rolled around, Sol claimed its first hour—the 25th in order. Thus the second day was Sol's day; likewise the third was Luna's, the fourth Mars's, and so forth. This method of enumerating and naming the days of a week was finally adopted by the Romans in the fourth century A.D., unchanged except that the day of Sol (*solis dies*, now Sunday), rather than the day of Saturn, was placed first. The rest, in order, were called *lunae dies*, *Martis dies*, *Mercurii dies*, *Jovis dies*, *Veneris dies*, and *Saturni dies*. The Romance languages all use derivatives of these names (compare the French *lundi*, *mardi, mercredi,* etc.), though Saturday is regularly renamed "Sabbath day" (as for example *sabato* in Italian) and Sunday "the Lord's day" (*domenica* in Italian).

Now, while it is true that the planets were originally named according to the notion that they actually manifested their nominal gods, such beliefs were long dead by the time the Romans instituted the week. When the old Germanic tribes in turn borrowed the Roman scheme, however, they presumed the days were named directly after gods rather than after the planets, and proceeded to substitute equivalent deities from their pantheon. *Solis dies* and *lunae dies* made the transition rather easily, since it involved merely the substitution of old Germanic words for "sun" and "moon." The resulting names passed into Old English as *sunnandaeg* and *monandaeg*, respectively, obvious equivalents of the modern "Sunday" and "Monday."

The other days, however, required some thought. For the Mars of *Martis dies*, the Germans substituted the Teutonic war-god Tyr, or Tiw, resulting in the Old English *tiwesdaeg*, "Tuesday." *Mercurii dies* presented more of a problem, since the Roman Mercury had no clear Germanic equivalent, but eventually the translators settled on Odin, a.k.a. Wotan and Woden, more nearly related to the Roman Jupiter but connected to Mercury by virtue of his being, among other things, the god of learning. The Old English word for Wednesday, therefore, was *wodnesdaeg*.

Having thus used up Odin, the Germans chose their thunder-god Thunor, also known as Thor and Thur, as a substitute for the thunder-wielding Jupiter, yielding *thursdaeg*, "Thursday." For *Veneris dies* the Old English translation was *frigedaeg* (Friday), derived either from the Teutonic love-goddess Freya (possessive "Frige") or, more likely, from their goddess-in-chief, Frigga.

The biggest problem was posed by *Saturni dies*, since there was no equivalent Teutonic god to be had; thus the Germans merely Germanized the original Latin name. The Old English result was *saeterdaeg*, "Saturday"—ironically preserving the one name of a Latin god the Romance languages have abandoned.

A few mythological references are also preserved in the English names for the months, which are directly derived from Latin and which most likely date to the Roman invasion of Britain. "January," for example, is named after Januar, the festival of Janus celebrated in that month [*see* p. 12]. "February" derives from *februum*, "ritual purification," referring in particular to the rituals of Lupercalia, celebrated in February and dedicated to the fertility-god Faunus, a.k.a. Lupercus [*see* p. 60]. "March," more simply, is like *Martis dies* named after Mars, and "May" after the goddess Maia, a daughter of Atlas. "June," finally, is indirectly named after the goddess Juno, the Roman equivalent of Frigga.

The other months are named after Caesars (Julius and Augustus) or numbers (September through December, the seventh through tenth months according to the old calendar), except for April, whose origins are obscure—though it may derive from the Latin verb *aperire*, "to open." Go figure.

FLOWERS AND TREES

Everybody knows that plants love the sun—as long as there's not too much of it; but in a number of classical myths, it's the sun who loves plants. Or rather, it's the sun-god's love that turns his lovers *into* plants. Nearly as amorous as his father Zeus, Apollo was not so successful a suitor; but his loss was often nature's gain, as many of the following stories will prove. Some of these tales are very ancient, but many seem to have been whimsical inventions of the poet Ovid as he padded out his *Metamorphoses*.

THE CYPRESS—This evergreen descends from an Asian prince named Cyparissus, a comely youth much admired by Apollo. One day, Cyparissus accidently killed his favorite stag, which so mortified the prince that he nearly died. But Apollo came to Cyparissus's rescue, transforming him into a tree in the nick of time. An odd way to save a lover's life, admittedly, but Apollo was an odd god.

THE HELIOTROPE—Though the name "heliotrope" is today most properly given to a small South African plant with purple flowers, heliotropes are generically plants that "turn to the sun," which is what their name means in Greek. And according to the Greeks, the original heliotrope was Clytia, a daughter of the Titans Oceanus and Tethys, and another in a long line of Apollo's lovers. Clytia and Apollo were a happy pair until the god laid eyes on the Assyrian princess Leucothoe. Abandoning Clytia and disguising himself as the Assyrian queen, Apollo went off to live at court with Leucothoe, leaving his jilted lover to plot revenge. The best she could do was expose Apollo's ruse to Leucothoe's father, but this was effective enough, since it caused the king to bury the princess alive. Even Apollo could not save Leucothoe from her fate, but by sprinkling nectar on the mound he raised her body in the form of a new tree, now known as the "frankincense" after the aromatic gum resin it "weeps." As for Clytia, she had not helped her cause by betraying Apollo, who only despised her the more. Abandoned and grief-stricken, Clytia sat alone for nine days and nine nights, eating nothing, forlornly watching her lover drive the sun across the sky. In the process, she took root in the ground and was transformed into the *heliotropion*, the flower that turns its head to the sun.

THE HYACINTH—Hyacinthus, an ancient Spartan prince, caught the fancy not only of Apollo but also of Zephyrus, a personification of the West Wind. This time Apollo's love was actually requited, which mightily ticked off his rival. One day, as the lovers amused themselves in a game of quoits, Zephyrus blew a discus Apollo had thrown so that it struck Hyacinthus on the head, killing him on the spot. The disconsolate sun-god raised a flower out of his lover's blood and placed the body among the constellations. On the petals of the flower, known in Greek as *hyakinthos*, Apollo inscribed the woeful cry, "AI" (alas!), which one may supposedly discern even to this day. But this *hyakinthos* is not the flower we call the hyacinth; it seems to have rather been a kind of iris, or perhaps a pansy. Which leads us to another story . . .

THE IRIS—Iris was the Greek name for the rainbow and also for its personification, the goddess Iris, the wife of Zephyrus and one of Zeus's messengers. But while the plant we call the "iris," which comes in a variety of gaudy colors, appropriately takes its name from the goddess, she has nothing else to do with it. In fact, our iris is probably the plant the Greeks called *hyakinthos*, which has two mythological origins. In one version, as we have seen, it was raised by Apollo from the blood of Hyacinthus; in the other, it sprang of its own will from the blood of the Greek warrior Ajax. As the story goes, after Prince Paris of Troy had slain Achilles [*see* p. 93], Odysseus bested Ajax in a contest for their ex-comrade's arms. His defeat drove the overweening Ajax mad; and after killing a flock of sheep he deliriously fancied were his Greek enemies, he committed suicide. From the bloody earth arose the plant *hyakinthos*, whose petals bore the cry "AI," etcetera.

THE LAUREL—Once upon a time, Apollo fell in love with a beautiful maiden named Daphne, a daughter of Gaia by the river Ladon and a devotée of the virgin goddess Artemis (Apollo's twin sister). The sun-god, however, had a formidable rival in the Pisan prince Leucippus, whom Daphne preferred. Since no man was permitted into the society of Artemis's followers, Leucippus disguised himself as a woman so he could enjoy Daphne's company; but the jealous sun-god exposed the ruse, and when Leucippus was discovered Artemis ordered him killed. As you might imagine, this didn't exactly warm Daphne's heart, and she fled the god in fear and loathing. When she could no longer outpace him, she prayed Zeus to deliver her; the god assented by changing her into the laurel tree (called *daphne* in Greek). So great was Apollo's love that thenceforth the laurel was sacred to him, and thus the tree became associated in Greece with prophetic and poetic inspiration. This is why a nation's greatest poets are its "poets laureate."

THE LOTUS—This story is a bit skimpy: the lotus plant was originally a nymph named Lotis who prayed to be changed into a flower so that she might avoid the lecherous advances of the god Priapus, a son of Dionysus. But at least the tale allows me to introduce the adjective "priapic," which now means "phallic"; the god Priapus was in fact a Greek personification of the erect penis. He was, naturally enough, a fertility god, taking particular care of vineyards, which were sacred to his father. He was later adopted as a guardian of gardens, where one might have found his image used as a scarecrow.

See also AN ECHO AND NARCISSISM (p. 55), AN ADONIS (p. 95), *and* MYRRH (p. 124).

THE ZODIAC

Though the word "zodiac" is originally Greek—from *zodiakos kyrklos*, "circle of little animals"—the Greeks stole the idea from the Babylonians, who had already determined that the sun passed through twelve "signs" whose figures—lion, ram, bull, and so forth—could be sketched out of the constellations by connecting the dots. But once the Greeks had appropriated the concept and most of the figures—most likely in the sixth century B.C.—they then came up with their own explanations of how all those animals and people had gotten into the sky.

Here are the twelve signs and their myths:

ARIES—Latin for "the Ram" (*Krios* in Greek), not to be confused with the war-god Ares. According to the Greeks, *Krios* was the friendly, talkative ram whose golden fleece inspired the legendary quest by Jason and the Argonauts [*see* p. 192]. Zeus placed the ram in the heavens after it had been sacrificed to him and skinned.

TAURUS—this constellation takes its name from the Greek *Tauros*, "the Bull," namely the bull who, at Zeus's bidding, carried Europa across the sea from Phoenicia to Crete. In the more popular version of the myth, the bull was Zeus himself [*see* EUROPE, p. 103].

GEMINI—"Gemini" is the Latin translation of the Greek *Didymoi*, "the Twins." A slew of candidates were suggested as Gemini's originals, but the only pair close to being true twins were Castor and Pollux—sons of Leda, but by different eggs. Confused? Then *see* p. 119.

CANCER—"the Crab" (*Karkinos* in Greek, *Cancer* in Latin); according to some one of Hera's pet monsters, crushed by Heracles in his second labor [*see* p. 111]. This constellation was originally known in Greek as "the Asses' Crib," upon which "the Crab" was certainly an improvement. However, given the Latin's unpleasant associations, Cancers would later be given the even more improved name "Moon Children."

LEO—Latin for "the Lion," called *Leon* in the original Greek. This beast was known on earth as the Nemean Lion, another of the pests Heracles had to dispose of [*see* p. 111]. This tale, however, begs the question of why Zeus would elevate such a menace to the zodiac; perhaps it was to placate Hera.

VIRGO—"the Virgin" in Latin, whose Greek name was *Parthenos*. This sign was supposed to represent any of a number of divine virgins, but the best candidate was Dike, Justice personified, removed from earth by her father, Zeus, after mankind had grown so degenerate that earthly justice became a joke.

LIBRA—Latin for "the Balance" or "the Scales," from the equivalent Greek word *Zygos*. This sign was originally called "the Claws," which were supposed to be attached to Scorpio; the later idea of a balance may derive from the relative equality of day and night at the autumnal equinox. At first Scorpio held the scales in his claw, but then they were transferred to Virgo, who used them to weigh competing claims and thus to dispense her justice.

SCORPIO—Latin for "the Scorpion" (*Skorpios* in Greek). This fearsome creature figured in an argument between the goddess Artemis and the legendary gigantic Greek hunter Orion. Vain of her own skill in the hunt, Artemis did not take kindly to Orion's boast that he could single-handedly kill every last animal on earth. She used her deadly scorpion to prove him wrong. Orion did, however, get to become a constellation himself as a consolation prize.

SAGITTARIUS—"the Archer" in Latin, called *Toxotes* in Greek. Sagittarius has always been represented as a Centaur with a bow, even though Centaurs were not known by the Greeks to arm themselves in this fashion. If Sagittarius is supposed to represent one Centaur in particular, who that might have been is now unknown; perhaps it was the wise and kindly Chiron, tutor to the heroes Achilles, Jason, and Asclepius.

CAPRICORN—*Capricornus* is a Latin compound of "she-goat" (*capra*) and "horn" (*cornus*), which translates the original Greek *Aigokeros*, "goat-horned." The name itself is hard to figure out, but the figure itself is harder, being a fish with the head of a goat. The fishy part of it is that Capricorn is supposed to have been the goat that fed the infant Zeus as he was secretly raised on Crete, the goat whose horn became the original "cornucopia" [*see* p. 182]. Where this animal got his strange body is not recorded in the myth.

AQUARIUS—called by the Greeks *Hydrochoös*, "the Water-Pourer," Aquarius was said by some to be Deucalion, the Greek Noah, who was (with his wife) the only survivor of a great prehistoric flood [*see* p. 100]. Why he was raised into the sky at death has not been explained, though perhaps it was his reward for restoring the human race—an achievement you'd think Zeus would have found dubious.

Others suggested that *Hydrochoös* was actually Ganymede, Zeus's cupbearer, which explains how Aquarius got his cup, but which doesn't explain why he's pouring water from it. "Aquarius" is a Latin translation of the Greek name.

PISCES—called *Ichtyes* ("the fishes") by the Greeks, "Pisces," again, being the Latin translation. This sign apparently bored the ancients, since they came up with no myth to explain it.

THE PANTHEON

Today "pantheon" is used mostly in the sense of "a grouping of the gods, or of god-like persons"—primarily the latter, as the ancient deities have given way to TV stars and sports heroes. But the word originally meant nothing of the sort; indeed, the ancient Greeks never used it at all. *Pantheion* (from *pan*, "all," and *theios*, "sacred to a god") was coined in later times to name a temple dedicated to all a nation's gods, the most famous such building being the Pantheon still on display in Rome. The word, once adopted through Latin into English, retained its original sense until the twentieth century, when the place-name was transferred to the beings worshipped there.

Far be it from me to buck a trend. Though a catalog of classical pantheons would no doubt fascinate, a catalog of gods will probably prove handier, especially if you've had a hard time keeping straight their various names, attributes, and genealogies. What follows is an alphabetical list of all the important players and their powers. Minor gods and heroes later elevated to godhood (such as Heracles and Asclepius) are excluded.

APHRODITE—Greek goddess of love, beauty, generation, and all the good things in life. She was born from the severed genitalia of Uranus and the foam of the sea. She would later be identified by the Romans with their goddess VE-NUS.

APOLLO—The Greek sun-god, child of Zeus and Leto (a daughter of Cronus). Most likely a god of herdsmen in origin, over time Apollo took on a whole slew of powers and functions; not only would he become a god of the sun, but also the god of poetry, music, prophecy, archery, medicine, youthful beauty, law, and philosophy. Apollo was, in short, the patron of nearly everything the Greeks associated with the advancement of civilization. The god was called Apollo by the Romans as well, though they often preferred his epithet PHOEBUS.

ARES—One of the younger deities, the son of Zeus and Hera, Ares was the Greek god of war. His most famous adventure, however, involves a humiliating and very un-warlike liaison with Aphrodite. Ares later lent his myths to the Roman god MARS.

ARTEMIS—Twin sister of Apollo and virgin goddess of wild lands; thus a huntress, famous for her ferocity not only toward beasts but also toward men who intruded on her sacred company. Known to the Romans as DIANA and also as PHOEBE (as Apollo was known as Phoebus).

ATHENA—Namesake and patron of the city of Athens, Athena was also the Greek goddess of cities in general, as well as of the various crafts which arose in those cities. This association later led to her identification as the goddess of wisdom. (She was thus understood by the Romans to be their goddess MINERVA.) Hesiod claims that Athena was the daughter of Zeus by his first wife, Metis (Wisdom); she was later said to have sprung full-formed out of Zeus's head when Hephaestus split it with an axe.

BACCHUS—*see* DIONYSUS.

CERES—The Roman version of DEMETER.

CHAOS—The most ancient of all beings, the original universal force and thus the ancestor of all the gods.

CRONUS—The greatest of Titans and the father by Rhea of the Olympian gods. Cronus was originally some sort of harvest deity, but he later became best known for his craftiness and was also said by some to be Father Time himself. The Romans attempted to assimilate Cronus to their own god SATURN.

CUPID—A Roman name for EROS.

DEMETER—The Greek corn-goddess and the ultimate patron of agriculture. Demeter was one of the original Olympians, in other words a daughter of Cronus and Rhea. She was known to the Romans as CERES.

DIONYSUS—The son of Zeus and the nymph Semele, Dionysus was the Greek wine-god and also a patron of the arts—or at least of the ecstatic, mystical, and irrational tendencies in art. He was also called BACCHUS, by which name he became known to the Romans.

ERINYES—*see* FURIES.

EROS—Said by some to be a very ancient deity, one of the original offspring of Chaos, Eros was the Greek personification of desire. The Romans knew him as CUPID and considered him Venus's ever-youthful son, a cherubic mischief-maker who terrorized men and women with his arrows of love and hatred.

FATES—*see* MOIRAI.

FORTUNA—The Roman goddess of chance, their equivalent of the Greek TYCHE.

FURIES—Three daughters of Uranus, born from the blood he shed on Gaia (like the Gigantes). Greek personifications of malediction, the Furies tormented the evil in Tartarus and effected curses on Earth. They were called ERINYES in Greek and *Furiae* in Latin.

GAIA—The Earth; the first child of Chaos and the mother of the Titans, Furies, and Gigantes. Called TELLUS and TERRA by the Romans.

GIGANTES—Huge and fierce offspring of Gaia by the blood of a castrated Uranus—thus their name, from *Gegenes*, "sons of Ge [Gaia]." (The Greek stem *gigant-* is the ultimate source of our word "giant.") The Gigantes made war on the gods but were defeated after Zeus recruited his son Heracles.

HADES—An original Olympian, son of Cronus and Rhea, granted by Zeus dominion over the underworld. Also a god of vegetal growth, Hades was euphemistically known as PLUTO, which later became his common name among the Romans.

HECATE—Daughter of the Titans Coeus and Phoebe and an ancient Greek goddess of women, closely associated (and often identified) with Artemis. Later known as a patroness of witchcraft.

HELIOS—An offspring of Hyperion; the old Greek sun-god, not to be confused with his successor Apollo. The Greeks also nicknamed Helios HYPERION after his father and sometimes thought of him as the sun itself. The Romans identified their sun-god SOL with Helios.

HEPHAESTUS—Greek god of fire and foundries, in Homer the son of Zeus and Hera but in later myths the son of Hera alone. Hephaestus, the oft-cuckolded husband of Aphrodite, supposedly hid his smithies in volcanoes, which take their name from his Roman counterpart VOLCANUS, a.k.a. VULCAN.

HERA—Principal Greek goddess, a daughter of Cronus and Rhea, and thus Zeus's sister as well as his last wife. Hera's domains included marriage and women's lives generally. Called JUNO by the Romans.

HERMES—Greek god of skill, commerce, eloquence, and cunning; Zeus's son and envoy; divine thief. His myths were later transferred to the Roman god MERCURY.

HESTIA—Greek goddess of friendly fire and of the hearth; an original Olympian goddess, a daughter of Cronus and Rhea. Her name and functions are related to those of the Roman hearth-goddess VESTA.

HYPERION—The sun in Greek mythology; one of the Titans (children of Uranus and Gaia). The name TITAN in the singular refers to Hyperion.

JANUS—An old Italian deity of unknown parentage, originally the guardian of doorways and later the god of boundaries and beginnings.

JUNO—The Roman equivalent of HERA.

JUPITER or JOVE—The Roman equivalent of ZEUS.

KORE—see PERSEPHONE.

MARS—Later identified with the Greek war-god ARES, Mars seems to have originally been an Italian earth-god, presiding in particular over spring, the beginning of the agricultural year.

MERCURY—The Roman god of commerce, whose mythology was largely borrowed from that of the Greek HERMES.

MINERVA—The Roman ATHENA, goddess of handicrafts and wisdom.

MOIRAI—The three Greek Fates, offspring either of Zeus and Themis (a daughter of Gaia) or of Night by her lonesome. Their names were Clotho, Lachesis, and Atropos; they dealt out and then cut off the thread of every person's life. The Fates were known to the Romans as PARCAE or *Fata*.

MNEMOSYNE—A Titaness, memory personified; known chiefly in Greek mythology as the mother, by Zeus, of the Muses.

MORS—"Death"; the Roman equivalent of THANATOS.

MUSES—Nine daughters of Zeus and the Titan Mnemosyne; at first largely anonymous, but later given the names Calliope, Clio, Erato, Euterpe, Melpomene, Polyhymnia, Terpsichore, Thalia, and Urania. Their function was to inspire poets and kings in particular and to patronize the arts and sciences in general.

NEMESIS—Fatherless daughter of Nyx (Night), Nemesis was a divine agent of justice and balance; her chief task was to cut down any mortal who started thinking too highly of him- or herself. Also called Nemesis by the Romans.

NEPTUNE—An Italian water-god, identified with the Greeks' POSEIDON.

NOX—The Roman NYX.

NYX—The goddess Nyx, Night personified, sprang directly out of Chaos; she was the progenitor of various dark forces, such as Thanatos (Death), Hypnos (Sleep), Momus (Mockery), Misery, Nemesis, the Moirai (Fates), the Keres (Avengers of Trespassing), Deceit, Sexual Love, Old Age, and Eris (Strife). Quite an accomplishment. She was known to the Romans as NOX.

OCEANUS—A Titan, the Ocean personified, described by Homer as a great river encircling the world, and by other poets as residing at the western extreme of the earth.

PAN—Greek god of herds and of animal fertility, goat-like in appearance and sometimes in behavior. His parentage is variously given, but he is usually said to be a son of Hermes. Pan went by the same name in Roman myth.

PARCAE—The Romans' name for the MOIRAI (Fates).

PERSEPHONE or KORE—The goddess representing the spirit of growth in corn and other grains; a daughter of Zeus and Demeter. Persephone—known to the Romans, thanks to their mispronunciation, as PROSERPINA—was carried to the underworld by Hades to be his wife; she would become the object of several failed rescue attempts.

PHOEBE—A Titaness, identified with the moon; also called Titanis. Her name later became an epithet of ARTEMIS/DIANA, in her aspect as a moon-goddess.

PHOEBUS—An epithet of APOLLO, in his aspect as sun-god.

PLUTO—A euphemistic name, later adopted by the Romans, for HADES.

PLUTUS—Son of Demeter by the hero Iasion; Greek god of bountiful harvests and thus of wealth in general. Sometimes identified with HADES, a.k.a. PLUTO.

POSEIDON—Greek god of the sea, son of Cronus and Rhea and thus one of the elder Olympian deities. Familiarly known as "Earth-Shaker," Poseidon was also the god of earthquakes, which in ancient Greece were supposed to have something to do with water. He was called NEPTUNE by the Romans.

PROSERPINA—The Roman name for PERSEPHONE.

RHEA—A Titaness, daughter of Uranus and Gaia, and an old Greek nature-goddess. By Cronus she was the mother of the Olympian gods. Also called Rhea by the Romans.

SATURN—An old Italian god of obscure provenance; identified with the Greek Titan CRONUS.

SOL—As a common noun, "the sun"; as a proper noun, the old Roman sun-god, identified with HELIOS.

TARTARUS—Described by Hesiod as a child, along with Gaia (Earth) and Eros (Love), of Chaos. Originally a vaguely conceived infernal landscape, Tartarus was later imagined as that portion of the underworld reserved for the wicked.

TELLUS or TERRA—Roman names for GAIA; also known as Terra Mater, "Mother Earth."

TETHYS—A Titaness, known only as the mother, by Oceanus, of the world's rivers.

THANATOS—The Greek god of death, sometimes death personified; said to be a son of Nyx and thus a more unpleasant brother of Sleep. Often paired in modern times (as by Freud) with Eros, Thanatos was known as MORS among the Romans.

TITAN—Another name for HYPERION.

TITANS—The elder Greek gods, sons and daughters of Uranus (the Sky) and Gaia (the Earth). Hesiod lists twelve Titans: Oceanus, Coeus, Crius, Hyperion, Iapetus, Theia, Rhea, Themis, Mnemosyne, Phoebe, Tethys, and Cronus. Titans with distinct functions are discussed individually in this catalog. Many of the Titans are now satellites of their brother, the planet Saturn.

TYCHE—The Greek personification of Fortune; a daughter of the Titans Oceanus and Tethys. Tyche is more central in

Roman myth, where she is known as FORTUNA, than in Greek.

URANUS or OURANOS—A son of Gaia (the Earth), Uranus is the sky or heavens in Greek mythology; he was the father by Gaia of the Titans, whom he imprisoned in Tartarus but who would later overthrow him. Having no equivalent in Roman myth, Uranus is an intruder among the nine planets, the rest of which are given Latin names. (Names of moons, however, are Greek.)

VENUS—Perhaps originally an Italian goddess of vegetal fertility, Venus, whose name meant "beauty," was later identified by the Romans with the Greek sex-goddess APHRODITE.

VESTA—Roman goddess of the hearth fire, the equivalent of HESTIA.

VULCAN or VOLCANUS—Italian god of destructive fire, especially volcanic fire; identified with the Greek god HEPHAESTUS.

ZEUS—Greek god of thunder, the son of Cronus and Rhea. Zeus took control of the skies and earth after toppling his father, though he would continue to have trouble controlling himself. Known to the Romans as JUPITER and JOVE.

INDEX

Words and phrases which head entries in this book have their principal page numbers given in *italics*. When a character is treated at length in one entry, the page numbers of that entry are also given in italics.